Hendrik Dinkelman and Jacoba Wachter,
Our Story

Wedding photograph of Hendrik Dinkelman and Jacoba Wachter

Hendrik Dinkelman and Jacoba Wachter, Our Story

Compiled by

Jan Dinkelman Crawford
Cynda Dinkelman Bowen

TEMPLE HILL BOOKS

ISBN 978-1-4341-0567-7
Copyright © 2024 Jan Dinkelman Crawford. All rights reserved.
Published by Temple Hill Books.

Contents

Introduction

This book is a transcript of the personal histories written by Hendrik Dinkelman and Jacoba Wachter, as well as the daily journal that was kept by Hendrik while on his mission to Holland.

As per Hendrik's instruction, "I have directed those who have typed my history to make very few changes or corrections as I felt the objective of my history was that the reader may know me as I am", very few corrections have been made to his original writings.

An index has been added to highlight the interesting stories, events, and thoughts that Hendrik and Jacoba experienced at various times in their lives.

On the last page of his journal, Hendrik expressed a wish to pass the following messages to his posterity:

"I hope this story may be of benefit to my posterity on the journey through life."
"May the Lord bless you and that you may benefit by the lessons that I have learned."

Origin of the name Dinkelman

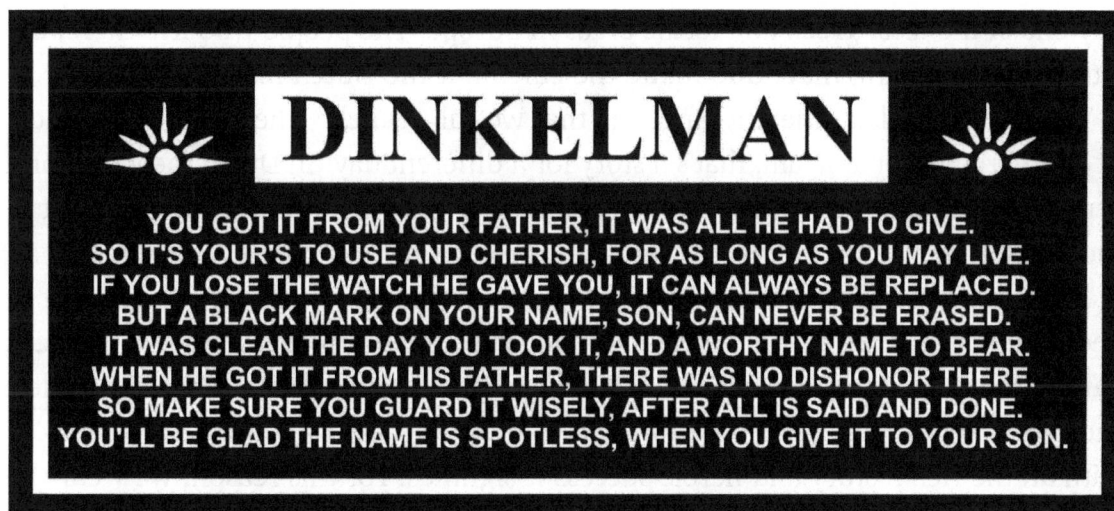

Americanized form of German Dinkelmann: occupational name for a grain producer or dealer, from Middle High German dinkel 'spelt, wheat'+man 'man'.

Dutch: altered form of German Dinkelmann (see 1 above), or possibly a habitational name for someone who lived at the river Dinkel in the Dutch-German border area of Twente.

Family Search, Dictionary of American Family Names© Patrick Hanks 2003, 2006

In the northwestern corner of Europe lies a sand expanse of marshy land which has long been subjected to the harsh winds and turbulent storms of the North Sea that regularly pound the large dunes that form a poor defense against the heavy tides and cold ocean currents of the cold. This land, called the "Nether"lands (or "Low"lands) by the people who lived on the "Upper"lands (or "high"lands) was seen as not a very desirable place to live. Since most of the Netherlands were below sea level, the land was little more than uninhabitable swamp and marsh.

Hundreds of years ago, some people living near the marshes thought that, if they could just build mounds of dirt high enough to keep the salty ocean tides from covering the fields, they could protect the lands and make them fertile. When this was successful, they devised a way to use the energy from the ocean winds to lift the water out of the lower lands and send it back to the ocean. This allowed for the "Lowlanders" or "Netherlanders" to reclaim their land and make the land productive and safe. This new land that was below sea level is called "Holland" and it is to this day one of the most green and fertile areas in Europe. The people who live there, the Dutch have a saying that "God made the earth but the Dutch made Holland."

The Dutch speak a different language that we call "Dutch" (they call it "Hollands" or "Netherlands") but again, that's a story for a different day! In Dutch the word for a certain type of grain is "dinkel." So when a farmer grew that grain and brought it to the market, he was known as the "man who brought dinkel" or the "Dinkelman." So many, many generations ago, an ancestor (or many ancestors) of ours, who fought to keep the ocean tides off the fields and make sure the grain could grow to harvest, earned the name "Dinkelman" and, while later generations of their descendants left the farms and, in our case, took to the sea, they kept the name of their ancestors with all the rich history and heroic success it signifies. For this reason, we wear the uncommon surname "Dinkelman" with pride.

Penned by John W. Dinkelman, grandson

Hendrik Dinkelman

Youth and Family of Origin

This is the history of Hendrik Dinkelman, who was born 23 of January 1898, in the city of Hilversum in the province of North Holland in the Netherland.

As a member of the Church of Jesus Christ, having been counseled to write the story of my life, for the benefit of my children, grandchildren, and all who may come after, hoping that it may help them on their journey through life. As I attempt to do so "being 84 years old," I seek the Spirit of the Lord to guide and direct me in this undertaking, It is my desire to write and to rewrite this record as true as my memory lets me, not seeking to glorify neither to conceal my weaknesses, mistakes, and failings.

I am born in humble circumstances being the fifth child of a family of five boys and five girls, [*Jan Frans 1891-1961, Frederik 1893-1967, Adriaan 1894-1949, Petronella 1896-1980,Hendrik 1898-1988, Geertje Alida 1899-1989, Johanna Berendina 1900-1996, Leendert 1902-1902, Antje 1904-1984, ? Dinkelman 1905-1905, Adriana 1907-1997 and Leendert 1908-1924*] all born and raised in a small home with little conveniences, such as no warm or cold water in the house, no bathroom and lack on space for such a large family.

My parents were hard working people giving their all to their children, of which I will always gratefully remember them. Though they have had very little schooling, yet they taught us to be thrifty, never to be wasteful, and above all to learn to work. Laziness was looked upon as a crime.

Besides his work as a railroadman, who in those early days were working 12 hours a day, he did grow all the potatoes, vegetables and pork for his large family.

Needless to say we boys were put to work even when we were very young, which never has done us any harm.

Mother, having that many children to take care of, was even taking in washing and ironing for well-to-do people to earn some money to supplement Father's wages, which were very low at that time. It is easy to understand that my sisters were not left idle either. For them too, there was always plenty to do to help Mother in the household. And when they did grow up and become wives and mothers, they too knew how to cook and sew and make a home.

Whenever I think back about my parents, I am amazed; working so hard and such long days and under such continuous stress to make ends meet, they could have lived to be ninety.

Our home was so small for such a large family and so few conveniences for Mother to do all her cooking in such a small kitchen, No wonder she prepared a whole meal in a big iron pot and we all got a plateful and it was a set rule never to leave any of the meal on the plate to be wasted, which sometimes, we tried to feed to the dog or cat under the table

As young as I was, I still remember the joy we as young children felt when the time came when we got running water in the house, even if it was just cold water, and what a joy when we got electric lights. Now we did not have to go outside to pump for water anymore. We began to feel like aristocrats, even though we never got hot water, neither a bathroom. But all our neighbors were in the same fix, and we did not feel that we were missing much.

Later in life I always did wonder how Mother has been able to keep us clean and well dressed. Of course, I having three older brothers, I have been wearing their clothing as much as it was possible. And still, do I remember the first complete suit I got new, when I was about ten years old. We did wear wooden shoes until we were twelve and got a job. Only on Sundays we did wear our leather shoes to Sunday School.

Saturday night was always the big cleanup night. That night all wooden shoes were scrubbed and we kids one after the other in the tub and clean night clothing on, and to bed.

Of course, to live and to be raised in such a crowded place, we at times had among us kids conflicting demands and ideas of interest and developing quarrels which were usually settled by mother saying "I will tell your Father." This was, as a rule, enough.

All in all, I like to think back upon my youth and home life with thankfulness for my parents, my brothers and sisters, for the good times we had singing and playing together. How we could appreciate when something new was bought. How we could be happy with so little.

The outstanding evening of the year was, for us kids, New Years Eve. Then Mother made all kinds of goodies and we were to stay up till midnight and could hear the church clock strike twelve. This was a solemn moment. During that night we could play all kinds of plays and sing all the songs we knew, especially the church songs Mother did like so much. As the night wore on, she became more emotional. She would go over all the things that has happened during the past year. The sickness we have had, the little accidents which has taken place. The many blessings we all have enjoyed and above all , the fact that we have stayed together and no one was missing. She could have a cry spell and we kids did the same but not for long. Yet we felt so close together, and after we all were filled up with goodies we went to bed after wishing each other a happy New Year.

One simple thing I do remember so well, yet it show how little favors can be remembered so long. Mother use to make bread dough and it was for sometime my job to take this pan with dough to the baker, who would then bake that bread and coming out of school at noon, to pick this up and take this home. As a reward she would cut the end crust of the fresh baked bread and put some molasses on it for me. After 75 years I can still remember how tasty it was.

I had three brothers and one sister older than I. And I remember by the time they were 12 they got a job and went to work to help to earn their keep. (This was all the schooling we got.) It was a normal thing that they brought their earnings home to Mother at the end of the week. To me, being about 9-10 years, was looking to the time I could do the same. Of course, I did not know what I was longing for. In later years, I began to realize what my brothers has been denied. They all had good heads to learn, even to learn a trade was very hard to get, because it took some money to go to trade school.

My eldest brother [*Jan Frans*] became a grocery boy, the second sold newspapers on the railroad station until he was old enough to get a job on the railroad, just like my dad: As soon as I was 12 years old, I got a job in a clothing store, as a delivery boy, making one guilder a week, from 8:00 a.m. to 6:00 p.m., six days a week. At noon, I got a glass of milk and two slices of bread. Yet it was with certain pride when I, for the first time, my first earned guilder, put in Mother's lap. This job lasted about seven months, but did not make me happy, as I was left alone in the storeroom so much.

As my brothers were working in the grocery business, I too got a job in a grocery store, delivering groceries on a bike with a basket up front. As I was so short, my short legs could not reach the pedals all around, the boss made some wooden blocks and I was called the grocery boy with the wooden pedals. This was not an easy job, for at a time I had a big load in the basket and going up hill it was pushing instead of riding. However, I was much on the road, instead being cooped up in a storeroom rolling up bolts of fabric.

Besides delivering, I sometimes could help customers, which made me feel important. I also had the job of filling shelves and kept the boxes full with several items such as brown sugar. In those days everything was put on the scale and weighed by ounces or pounds, very few items were prepacked. With all that stuff laying around, it was hard for me to keep my fingers out of the brown sugar box or out of everything that was agreeable to my stomach. This job paid two and one half guilder, about one dollar, a week but the hours were that much longer.

This was altogether too much for this skinny boy of 13. No recreation to speak of, too tired to play in the street with other boys. I did not develop, too much rundown most of the time.

During that time I did develop a strong desire to go to sea. This was all I could dream about. It was thrilling sight for me when I saw a sailor in a neat uniform. However, I had to wait til I was 14. And after overcoming much resistance, Dad took me, on April first 1912, to the recruiting station, which just happen to be the navy. It would have made no difference to me to go navy or merchant marine, I did know no difference, yet after passing my physical test, I was the happiest boy in the world.

Religion in our home was taught mostly by Mother, who was more religious than Dad, who never went to church as far as I know. Yet in his older years, he was reading the bible regularly. I attended Sunday School for little kids. We always had to ask the blessing for the food, and before going to sleep, we kneeled to pray for protection during the night. Although Mother did not go often to church, yet all of us were baptized in the Dutch Reformed Church. This was one thing even non-church goers believed in very strong, because a child not being baptized was looked upon as a heathen.

I believe I was more religious inclined than any of my brothers. Maybe a little more curious in my thinking. As I, even as young as I was, had many questions which as a rule were far beyond my age to understand. Yet I had a strong belief in prayer. Why one should have more faith in prayer than others, I don't know, as we were all trained the same, under the same influence. Only in later life I began to see why questions such as: Is there really an all knowing almighty God, somewhere high in the sky? Is there really life after death? Looking up in the sky asking myself is there really a purpose in all those heavenly bodies? And for many of this kind of question, which were all beyond my comprehension, which I believe is normal for young people. Yet one would be surprised to know what can be revealed to young people who diligently, are seeking for true answers and understanding through sincere prayer. I have never had any doubt in the existence of a supreme being, I instinctively believed in life after death and as I grew older the question of the real purpose of our life upon this earth, became more clear to me.

At the time I was 10-11, I was over active, an abundance of energy made me do many things which were above my physical strength, which caused a breakdown and I became very sick. After recovering, I became a fervent reader. I always could be found with something to read. I always loved books, especially those which will bring tears to the eyes. Geography I loved to read about, and I loved to read comical stories to make me laugh.

From the time I was 4-5 years old I developed faith in prayer, which has stayed with me all my life. I always was trusting the Lord. He would give me an answer, childlike these prayers are, yet so important to a young child. Yet something happened that almost shattered my faith in prayer. But as it is with all of us, we need to learn how and for what we are praying. This lesson I learned when I was about 10-11 years old.

We had in our home my uncle who was a military man and to whom I was very much attached. I guess on account of his uniform, which made me look up to him. He became very ill, and with all the trusting faith, I went in the woodshed to pray for his recovery. Yet he passed away and I remember so well how disappointed I was. The Lord did not answer my prayer as I wanted. Yet later on as I was told that his passing away was a blessing in disguise. From that time on I learned to say "If it be thy will," having faith that the Lord knows best. Later in life, as I had many times an opportunity to administer to the sick, and making our desires known and pronouncing a blessing to say "but thy will be done in all things." Sometimes we need to exercise patience and waiting on the Lord for an answer.

My eldest brother [*Jan Frans*], who was seven years older as I, was always looked up to as the one who could answer my questions and was willing to help me to get the things done. He understood better than any of us the struggles of our parents and the beginning of their marriage life. As a young man he learned about the stresses of life and I remember him as one who had a calm nature and was always helpful to our younger ones. In later years I have felt close to him. I have for long the feeling he never could rise to his potential, partly health and partly a less successful marriage. He died a terrible death after a long suffering sick bed at the age of 70.

My next brother [*Frederik*] was altogether a different person. He was in many ways the right hand for Mother, always willing to do jobs for her and was a big help for Father in working on the land raising foodstuff, such as potatoes, beans, etc. He was the one who was called to peel the spuds because nobody could peel as thin as he. I also remember when he got out of school, he started his own business. I was only 8 years old and was his helper. Stacking up the briquette was just like building blocks, which I loved to do. As he went around the neighborhood, finding customers, what joy as he came back and had a few orders to deliver. This was, of course, penny business, but how rich he felt as he could give Mother the profit. He became just like Dad, a railroad worker and had that job 33 years. When he retired, he enjoyed his pension for about 20 years. Being a victim of the cigarette, he passed away at the age of 73, could have lived another 15-20 years.

My third brother [*AdriaanI*], too, was a different type of person, early more world wise than the others. Wise in some ways to wiggle himself out of work, that was left upon us kids. When he got out of school, he too got work in the grocery business, and seeking his way to a livery stable to satisfy his love for horses and before long, he worked himself in this line of business, and became the driver of the horse driven carriage, just like a cab driver today. This was his glory driving the two horses and the same time making more money than his brothers, but he also knew how to spend it, easy come, easy go. Being among those mostly rough and also drinking fellows, he knew the ways of the world before his time. He was the brother who instilled in me the desire to go to sea, as that was, for sometime his desire. But he pulled back and in time, I went. He, making good money, could at times buy us little kids cookies or candy and we loved him for it. Yet he did not take care of himself as he should and after spending some years in the infantry service during the first world war, his health, through heavy cigarette smoking and neglect, passed away when 55 years old.

All the menfolk in the family were heavy cigarette smokers, except Dad, he stayed with his pipe or cigar and blow the house full with smoke but not in his lungs. He lived till 90,which proves again that the cigarette is the mean killer of tobacco users.

My sister[*Petronella*] one and a half years older as I, was the first girl in the family. She was Father's pride, and she was always on his side. She was very sharp and was bossing us whenever she got the chance. She had all the attributes of a business women, which she, after marriage, could go into. She, in her growing teenage years, could at times go over the head of Mother and gave conflicts. She also was taken a job as maid servant which took her away from home. She was strong willed and after getting married and had two girls, one took after Dad and one took after Mother, a condition which brought much disharmony as long as they were married. She passed away after being a widow for a number of years at the age of 84.

Of my younger sisters I can't write too much. They were yet too young and I, leaving home when only 14, lost contact to a great extent with the family as a whole. Only I like to mention one of my younger sisters who had some physical difficulties and was at times abused and ridiculed on account of her difficulties, which she could have no control over. From the time we were very young, I had compassion for her and to defend her. We have stayed close all our lives.

My youngest brother [*Leendert*] [, 10 years younger as I, was six when I left home. He was our baby brother and loved by all of us. Being the youngest boy and did grow up under better economic conditions was the one who was going to trade school and was going in the mechanical field. However, he got lung cancer and died at 16 years old. This was the first loss in the family, which was very hard for Mother, as she loved her youngest son so much. This loss brought us closer together. This boy was very religious and his passing away, he was so completely ready to go to the other side.

One more girl was born who never has been blessed with children which she loved so much and wanted so bad. Yet she in later life has given all her love to elderly people and has done much good. She also got more schooling as we older ones. Born when things were getting so much better.

Two more sisters I have not mentioned, both are still living at the time of this writing, 1982. One was born on my birthday,[*Antje Dinkelman]* which made her some special to me.

As I read this over, one may (I am afraid) get the idea that I have been writing in a negative way. I am just writing as I remember my early impressions before I reach the age of 14. Beside our individual weaknesses, we could have so much fun, as the bunch came together, teasing one another, telling funny stories, sorrow when someone was sick or had an accident, rejoicing with those who had successes or a promotion. Yes, there was much good among this large family. Father and Mother lived to be ninety and have received a great deal of honor for the way they raised their 10 children in the circumstances as they were in those early days.

Oh how I wish I could have done more for them when in later years I was in the position to do so. But the ambition to excel in my work made me sometimes self-centered and let my chances to do some pleasant thing for them pass by, which I will regret as long as I live. Not that I was neglectful intentionally, oh no, but that great weakness of procrastination which is the one of the most successful tools of the devil.

Just a few lines about our neighborhood. We had a Jewish family as our neighbor. They were very poor but lived up to their faith. It was my privilege to be their help on Friday night and Saturday morning. I was to make a fire, to get warm water, to light their lamp and to keep the heater going when it was cold in winter. Saturday morning it was my job to blow out the oil lamp and to make a fire in the stove. I got 10 cents for my work, but it was a great experience to me. And as I did grow older and became more interested in the Jewish people and their history and their stubborn refusal of Jesus Christ, I could think often of those poor neighbors I remember in my youth.

Our neighborhood was just like a large family, always helping one who was in need, always finding a place to stay when one of the women was getting a baby, always getting something to eat when Mother was in bed. In those days the children were born in the home, and as soon as we were boarded out of got some kids in our home we know the time had come for another sister or brother.

As I already mention before, I was a lad of 9-10, very active. I would like to say over active mind, which found its outlet in helping Father raising hogs. In the spring, Father would buy about 3-4 weaner pigs, so that in the fall he would have one to kill for the family and the others to sell for cash. This hog raising had the interest of me to the extent that all my energy was directed to taking care of those hogs. For bedding, I could go out and rake leaves to keep them warm and dry. We had a big iron pot to cook potato peels and small potatoes and everything from the land that was edible for hogs. They had to be raised the most economical way possible. It was, in my eye very important that there was always of potato peels on hand to cook. Gradually, I was building up among the neighbors a potato peel round, and as soon as I came out of school, I did pick up a gunny sack and gathered those peels which the people left for me to pick up, not only the peels but anything that was good for hogs to eat. After all these years, I remember so well how disappointed I could be as some of a large families were eating rice instead of potatoes that day. Also I remember the Mondays which was a double day and at times was more as I could carry in on trip. And the joy and satisfaction as Dad praised me as being his big help. At that age, when I was asked what I was going to be, my answer was always, I was going to be a farmer or hog raiser, which 20 odd years later became a reality in this country.

This winds up the story of my life, the first 14 years. Leaving home at that age for my eighteen year navy career and loosing much contact with my family.

This picture Taken in 1916

1. Jan Frans   Passed away at the age 70
2. Frederik   "   "   "   "   74
3. Adriaan   "   "   "   "   75
4. Petronella   "   "   "   "   84
5. Hendrik
6. Geertje Alida
7. Johanna Berendina
8. Antje   "   "   "   "   " 80
9. Sjeane Adriana
10. Leendert   Passed away at the age 86
Dad   "   "   "   "   90
Mother   "   "   "   "   90

Family Life   Members of

MY NAME **Dinkelman Jan** BIRTH DATE **8 NOV 1867** DEATH DATE **1 NOV 1957**
SPOUSE'S NAME **Weideman Johanna B** BIRTH DATE **19 June 1872** DEATH DATE **30 Nov 1962**

CHILDREN	BIRTH DATE	PLACE OF BIRTH	D	EYE COLOR	HEIGHT	BODY BUILD*
Jan, Frans	23.9.1891	Hilversum	6.2.1961		M	M.
Johanna van Klingeren						
Frederik	13.2.1893	Hilversum	9.2.1967			M
Maria Post						
Adriaan	25.4.1894	Hilversum	15.4.1949			M
Sientje van Klingeren						
Petronella	27.7.1896	Hilversum	24.7.1980			M
Simon de Waal						
Hendrik	23.1.1898	Hilversum	[DOD- 22 November 1988]			M
Jacoba Wachter						
Geertje. ALida	28.6.1899	Hilversum	[DOD-19 April 1989]			M
Adriaan Kolman						
Johanna, Berendina	30-12-1900	Hilversum	[DOD-24 Mar 1996]			M
Louwerens Beuk						
Antje	23.1.1904	Hilversum	1984 [DOD-18 NOV 1984]			M
Marinus. N. Henny						
Leendert	10.12.1902	Hilversum	16.12.1902			
Adriana	6.4.1907	Hilversum	[DOD- 13 SEP 1997]			M
Jurian van Doorn, 2nd Frans van Oostenryk						
Leendert	21.8.1908	Hilversum	30.1.1924			

(S = Slender, M = Medium, L = Large)

COMMENTS OR PHOTOS

A SIMPLE DIRECT ANCESTRY THROUGH MY FATHER'S LINE

Hendrik Dinkelman 1893   Jan. Dinkelman 1867   Jan Frans Dinkelman 1820
MYSELF   MY FATHER   MY GRANDFATHER

Antje Elisabeth Dinkelman 1793   Jan Frans Dinkelman 1751   Johan Heirich Dinkelman 1715
MY GREAT GRANDFATHER   MY 2nd G. GRANDFATHER   MY 3rd G. GRANDFATHER

Arend Frans Dinkelman 1686   Henrich Dinkelman 1642
MY 4th G. GRANDFATHER   MY 5th G. GRANDFATHER   MY 6th G. GRANDFATHER

A SIMPLE DIRECT ANCESTRY THROUGH MY MOTHER'S LINE

Hendrik Dinkelman 1898   Johanna B. Weideman 1872   Frederik Weideman 1845
MYSELF   MY MOTHER   MY GRANDFATHER

Berend. Weideman 1800   Gerrit Jan Waideman 1750   Egbert Weideman 1725
MY GREAT GRANDFATHER   MY 2nd G. GRANDFATHER   MY 3rd G. GRANDFATHER

MY 4th G. GRANDFATHER   MY 5th G. GRANDFATHER   MY 6th G. GRANDFATHER

This picture taken 55 anniversary 8 apr 1946

My Father has worked on the railroad from his sixteenth jear till he was fifty six, and retired on account of his hearing. He has been a hard worker all his life. He lived untill he was 90 jear old – lost his Dad when seven and have had very little schooling. Mother has had a hard life. became a orphan when 13 and has born 11 children and raised 10 worked long hours to keep us clean and taught us to pray and have faith. She also has had very little formal schooling. She also like my Dad passed away when she was ninety –

These are my Father and Mother and my Brothers and Sisters

1 JAN FRANS

2 FREDERIK

3 ADRIAAN

4 PETRONELLA

5 HENDRIK

6 GEERTJE-ALIDA

7 JOHANNA-BERENDINA

8 ANTJE

9 ADRIANA

10 LEENBERT

Family Life — Activities

Included in this section should be those things which apply to the family as a unit when you were a child. Record those things that a person does in connection with his home or with his family. Try to record things that will tend to accentuate the positive aspects of home life. It is realized that all homes have some conflict between family members, but a de-emphasis of negative relations between family members would probably better suit the purpose for which one writes his history. Where contention must be mentioned, let it not embarrass anyone or work to destroy whatever family harmony exists. God's goal is to unite families. Let this personal history be written with that goal in mind.

MY FATHER'S CAREERS *I know very little about my Fathers early life exept he was born in humble circumstanses being the fifth child of his Fathers second Wife, who married him with three little children. His Father passed away when he was eight year old. Had very little schooling, and went to work on the railroad when 16*

MY MOTHER'S CAREERS *Mother being the oldest of nine children lost her mother when 13 and lost her Father when 15. got married when she was 19 and bore eleven children of who she raised 10 – 5 boys-5 girls. Has worked hard all her life, all her Brothers and Sisters has been raised in a orphanage Dad and Mam lived to be 90*

FAMILY ECONOMIC CONDITION *Every working mans economic condition, and with hard work and trift raised theyr children as suesesfull citizen, although none of theyr children reseived any kind of aducation beyond the age of Twelve. Dad has enjoyed his pension for Thirthy Four year.*

FAMILY TRADITIONS *Hard work. Trift an honesty, was the set rule in our home to waste any thing was looked upon as a sin*

My Sister and I. had this privilege to make the trip from Utah To attend This anniversary in the house we were born. This was a joy and surprice to them

65th Anniversary 11 april 1891 – 11 april 1956

"Fritz" [Frederik] Henk's brother's Family
circa 1950

Johanna and Jan with 2nd generation April 1936

Sisters Petronella, Johanna, Geertje

Hendrik with his parents and two unidentified family members
During Mission to Holland

Hendrik [Henk] and Johanna Berendina [Aunt Annie] arrive to
suprise their parents for their 60th Trovwdag [wedding day]

Moeder en Vader Dinkelman

On the first visit of Jacoba to her future husband's family
circa 1924
[taken from back of photo]

Johanna Berendina Weideman and Jan Dinkelman 60th wedding anniversary
April 1951

My Career as a Sailor and Navy Flyer

1912-1930

My desire to become a sailor became a reality on the first of April 1912. I was then 14 years and 3 months old and signed up for eight active and three reserve years, however that eight years started to count by the time I was 16.

This was the beginning a very successful and exciting career which lasted from 1912 until 1930. Dad took me by train to the city of Leiden, a well known old city, where the training school for young boys for the navy was located.

There, I started an all together different life, being full of ambition and feeling so well in these strict ruled daily activities, which kept us too busy to get homesick. The simple but good food, the exercise, the great variety of activities, that early to bed and early rise, made me grow and develop as a weed. Straight as an arrow and proud as a peacock wearing that sailor uniform, feeling I had the world by the tail, as yet not knowing what salt water tasted like.

After six or seven months coming home on my first furlough, the folks could not believe their eyes. Instead of that rundown grocery boy with drooping shoulders and knock knees, there was a happy sailor boy. So proud, so straight, he could only look at the stars. They sure taught us to keep the head high.

We got some schooling, the three R's. We had to learn to do our own washing and learn to sew and keep our own clothing in good repair. In short, to learn to take care of ourselves. Especially washing our own clothing was for us boys the tough thing, because it was all done by hand and every piece of clothing was inspected before it was put in the dryer. To help us in this job, we tried to keep ourselves as clean as possible. Washing machine was unknown. The strict discipline kept us out of trouble

19

with other fellows because it was considered to learn to get along and be helpful very important, as we would be living in close contact on board of ship with one another.

One thing we had no pleasure in, after all the good things we were taught for our physical well being, our spiritual well being was not overlooked. So Sunday morning, all dressed in our best clothes, we stood in line to go to church. First the Catholic boys apart, then the Protestants, it did not matter whether you were Lutheran or any other kind of denomination, this whole group went to one of the oldest churches in that city.

We were put away in a far corner, and boy was that two hours long. Sitting on a hard bench and listening to that long drawn out singing and preaching of the minister of things we could not have interest in. Continually watched by the leader of the group to prevent any kind of disturbance. Yet we made fun and tried to imitate, irreverently, the minister, or we could, ourselves, occupy with a needle to prick holes in a post card or something. It was also a trial as any of us needed to go to the boys room, because there was not any, and did we run as we came back to school. And what a relief when we heard the last amen. No wonder as soon as we were old enough to decide for ourselves, very few kept on going. And although church as such did not mean anything to me, yet I always remained prayerful as I was taught at home as a young child. Always before going to sleep I silently would say my prayers. First I was used to it and believed in prayer, second I had so much to ask for. Always asking to be able to do things well we were taught and with all the ambition and interest I had I did well.

The one activity we loved so much was the weekly trip we made with the long boats. They were long boats with 12 towers and getting away from the school and rowing through the canals, sometimes to other towns, going under those bridges and be encouraged by the people made it all worthwhile. I always remember the kettle of pea soup (snert) that was taken with us, and at noon was eaten somewhere on shore. How good it was to us boys after such a tough exercise on those oars.

This is the end of my first eight months of boot training. However, it would not be complete without writing some about the financial side of my story.

We started out with 160 guilder debt for all our clothing and bedding. We made 10 guilder a month. They took eight for paying our debt, one guilder was laid aside for train fare to go home on a furlough. This left us one guilder for the four weeks each month, or 25 cents. If we wrote a letter to our folks it cost five cents, if we needed an extra piece of soap, that was five cents, if we sent some postcards, five cents. Many times (Sunday afternoon) from one to five, we were free to go outside the gate. We usually went to the soldiers home to play some games. We got a cup chocolate for one penny and a slice of cake for two pennies. This done twice was about all we had to spend. To pay our debt took a long time, because if we needed to replace some piece of clothing or needed to resole our shoes, it went on our bill. I remember it was about three and one half years before I got my full earnings to spend myself.

In December 1912, we as a group of sixty boys were transferred to Hellevoetsluis, a town laying on the seashore to receive further training for the next one and a half years.

We were housed on an old three mast war vessel which was very impressive to us. In our minds we could see those old sailors, sitting high in those tall mast doing their duty in stormy weather, something we never would have to do. These were things of the past. However, my wife's father made three tours on those three mast frigates to Dutch East Indies and did tell us so much about life on those vessels. This ship was not in active service anymore but those gunport and those long decks below was to us so impressive.

Our training in seamanship and in small weapons was the main part of our boot training. The last three months we sent away on a sailing vessel what was usually used by the pilots on the open sea. Those three months of training was the climax as we were feeling like real seaman.

At the end of our boot training, some prizes were given to the highest students. The first prize being a silver watch. Somehow, I can't say exactly why, I began to ask the Lord that if it would be his will, I might receive this silver watch. Secretly perhaps the desire to receive praise from my folks and give evidence of my progress to become a real seaman. This watch was to me something as a real treasure and me asking in my prayers was almost second nature for a number of months, and I hope I did not tire the Lord.

When the time came, we were set up in a square. The commanding officer was giving an impressive talk about us being ready to go to an active warship to serve the queen in defending our Vaderland. This was for me so impressive I forgot all together about the desire I had to be eligible for that watch for which I had secretly prayed for so long. Yet when time came, it was with a shock to me when I heard my name called to come forward and be given, with a short speech, that silver watch. I do not remember that speech, but I sure remember my shaking knees and taking my place in the line. I could cry from thankfulness to the Lord, when I looked at that, to me, such a wonderful watch. Only then I became aware of the fact that the Lord had seen fit to answer my prayer. And I believe now more than ever before that the Lord answers sincere prayers. Not always as we wanted to but always in a way that would be to our good, if we only are willing to see the hand of the Lord in all things.

And so it is in seeking the truths of the gospel plan. In seeking for knowledge and answers for all our questions which come to our minds, for understanding of these three questions which are in the mind of so many of us. First, where did I come from? Second, what is the purpose of this mortal life? Third, where am I going?

Before we were transferred to an active warship, we had a furlough to see our folks and when I saw the pride of my parents after showing them my prize, this was my greatest reward, and I did appreciate my folks more than ever before.

July 1914, we as a group of 16-17 year old sailor third class, we found ourselves as green horns on a 5000 ton cruiser, and among these older and experienced seaman. We, for a short while, would be looked upon as green horns which did hurt our pride and we followed soon in habits such as smoking and using man language spoken by these older sailors. Swearing was not so bad as this was punishable. But there was plenty going around that did run against my up bringing.

This cruiser was mainly used for training purposes, but when only after one month the first world war broke lose, and although we were never actively involved, yet it changed the whole life and purpose of our ship. Now we were on war duty out on the open sea, traveling up and down along the coast in all kinds of weather. Defending our neutrality being surrounded by warring nations and were very much affected by it. We were totally moblized and could be pulled in anytime. Holland being a seagoing nation were shut off so much in our trade with India and other nations, we lost so many merchant ships on account of those floating mines. Many fisherman lost their lives and ships for getting those mines in their nets.

As time went on everything had to be rationed and many were going hungry. Being in the service we got enough food, but the variety was very much simplified. From July 1914 until March 1915, serving on this cruiser we young sailors running continually the sea watch, which is four hours up and eight hours off. But during the day there was plenty to do and to train. This was very hard for us young fellows. We were always on the go and not enough rest. Even when coming up the harbors it was with all speed loading coal, loading foodstuff and out to sea again. Yet so many things did happen and we felt so important, so much excitement, that we forgot how tired we were.

This time of my life, being exposed to the influence of those older seamen, many who had made several stints to tropical countries, all I ever learned about sex has come through those channels and surely was not very conducive to learn and to understand the great principles of chastity. The language of these older seamen was not helpful to us, and although using the name of the Lord in vain was strictly forbidden yet we picked up many words you would not use in church neither around women, words and expressions I never knew did exist. Almost over night we were transformed from boys to men. Still by being prayerful and finding support in my belief in a God helped me so much in staying more or less in a straight path. I did start smoking, but never started to drink,and was too shy to look to girls at that time. I had no time for that.

Some of my experiences as a young sailor I always will treasure for example the first time I was called to take my turn at the helm wheel. To stand there trying to keep that cruiser on course, I felt I was the most important person on the ship. But, of course, standing for two hours on the same spot and all the time the officer looking over my shoulder took the glory away in a hurry. The turn as a lookout high up in the crow nest was more exciting, to see the ship working its way in rough sea, seeing the nose of the ship dive under a big wave and coming up again like a dolphin. Of course, the movements high up are so much greater than below and thus no help for those who are suffering of seasickness. The job up there is to report anything that comes over the horizon, any light or mast or land.

In the spring of 1915, we were transferred as a group to the island Vlieland, north of Holland, to build a kind of stronghold and running watch along the shore, looking for things that came floating on shore, such as lumber from torpedoed ships or sunk by floating mines. Sometimes those floating mines came on shore and had to be blown up by a special crew, which was always an excitement for us. Dead bodies were found more than once. And so we were soldiers instead of seaman, digging trenches and setting up heavy guns. I have enjoyed the year and a half on that island.

Plenty of fresh air, lots of recreation, such as soccer ball and fishing and different kinds of sports which did all of us young fellows much good.

Some days we were kept busy salvaging a lot of stuff from ships that were sunk by submarine or mines. This was hard work but still interesting as you could see the great variety of articles that floated on shore. We also began to realize the unbelievable destruction of war. In our free hours we set out long fish lines with baited hooks by low tide and gathered the fish by high tide, which gave us some extra on the table.

Though I have enjoyed the time on this island. I was kind of anxious to be a sailor again. And after being promoted to sailor second class, I was glad to be transferred to a panserhip, the name was Kortenear, named after an early admiral who fought Spaniards in early days. I served on the ship eight months, was promoted to seaman first class, volunteered for the submarine service, was placed on the 05 only a 500 ton placement with the capacity of only four torpedos, total crew 11 men. I was the lowest in rank and was a helper for all trades but master of none.

I could write many sheets of paper with all the experiences of the two and one half years I served on this boat. Submarine living is not an easy life, but it pays so much more. My duties were quite a variety during traveling. I was the helmsman on the vertical rudder, when time came for dinner it was for me to serve the crew, coming or leaving the harbor my place was on the after deck to moor or to release the mooring lines. After shooting off a torpedo for practice, it was my job to crawl inside the tube to dry and then to grease the tube with heavy grease. This was a nasty job I had no liking for.

Sometimes going out for practice shooting, I was left behind to run the motor boat which was used to pick up the torpedo which was shot at a certain target. When the torpedo did run its course she would float to the surface, and it was my job to pick the torpedo up and get it back to the sub. This was responsible job, I had to watch continually for the track of the torpedo. Chances were to lose it and would be lost with the current.

We usually made day trips for training purposes. Traveling under the surface three-four hours, which made it necessary to charge the batteries again. Yes those old time submarines are a far cry compared to the latest subs that travel for weeks at a time and are having a crew of several hundred.

After traveling submerged for four hours the air was getting bad, no way to refresh, only after rising to the surface. We were housed on a mothership which has all the supplies and the sleeping quarters. I was paid two guilder for every hour we traveled submerged. This was attractive as my wages as seaman first class was not very much. This extra pay was not much either taking in consideration the danger in those old time subs.

These boats had no water tide compartment. If for some reason the boat could not be raised, there was not much chance to be rescued. There was a little steel buoy on top of the deck which could be turned lose, which was connected with a cable. If found it could be opened up and by telephone make communication. However, as young as I was, I saw no danger. I guess the excitement and adventurous nature made me overlook any kind of danger.

During the general maneuvers we were sent out for three days being on our own. During the day taking part in those maneuvers and during the night lay the boat on the seafloor for anchor. We would go down about eight p.m. and rise at six a.m. This was a test for the crew for endurance. This we did three nights in a row. One man to watch the instrument for one hour, the rest laying down. After the third night we were very much weary, getting back to base, I slept, I believe, for 24 hours. But the extra money I made it all worthwhile.

On this boat I had my most lucky experience. We had to stay overnight in the harbor of Den Helder, the navy base. As we were tied with our mooring line to another sub, who was tied with their lines to the shore, only four men, the lowest rank were kept on board to watch. It was a very stormy night and fast running current. The lines tied to the shore parted and these went, breaking our lines. The current took us out in the open.

One of the fellows knew how to start the electric motor and it was up to me to steer the boat back to the shore, before we would be beached with that high tide on the shallows. As I steered the boat up stream out of danger, the captain and the rest of the crew were standing on the shore and asked if I could bring back the boat to shore. Yes, if some mooring lines were ready.

I slowly maneuvered the boat back to place and without any damage, the boat was back. The captain, very pleased with the way I was able to handle the ship and was full of praise. I was a one hour sub captain, two weeks later, I was promoted to boatsman mate. This was for me a rich experience and has helped in later years. I am also thankful that in time of emergency I have proven to remain calm and has the presence of mind to do the best move for the occasion.

During those two and one half years I have 384 hours traveled under the surface, which was quite a number of hours for that time. As I remember the number of floating mines I have seen pass by, I am grateful to the Lord for his protecting care during the years of the war. After the armistice was signed, I was sent for my first stint to the Indies.

Leaving Holland Aug. 1919 for the Indies, facing a whole new way of life. Hoping to find a place on the only sub that was there, but was placed on a mine layer stationed at the most northerly part of the island of Sumatra. The ship with a crew of 80, half of them native Javanese. Learning to speak their language and get acquainted with my duties, which were all new to me. I served on this vessel eight months. My job was, beside the regular watch, running the motor boat between ship and shore, as the ship was always laying for anchor in the middle of the bay, those eight months has been most pleasant.

Every two or three weeks we would make a cruise along the west coast of the island, visiting oil refineries, plantations, stopping at many of those towns for showing the Dutch flag. As a crew of a Dutch warship we were always pleasant entertained and which was by us very much appreciated. One time we were taken to a place where they harvested the most expensive wood. It was black and it would not float. It was called ironwood mostly used for the tourist trade.

One of these trips I never will forget. During the monsoon, we were visiting the very important city Padang, laying in the bay for anchor for eight days, haven't seen the sun once, never knew it could rain so much and so long. Beside the benefit of have so much fresh water for washing our clothing it was plenty tiresome, and of course, seeing the city was altogether out of the picture. Those eight months on the mine layer was almost a long vacation.

One day a notice was put on the bulletin board, asking for three volunteers within a certain age, with rank of corporal, to be trained in the navy flying service as navigator and gunner. I did fit the required age and rank and, adventurous as I was, I turned in my name and after a few days, I received notice that I was one of the three chosen volunteers. After a replacement arrived, I was shipped back to Batavia on the island Java. This took eight days with a merchantship that made a stop at every town on the east coast of Sumatra for loading or unloading passengers and all kinds of commodities. Overloaded with passengers, men, women and children laying on several decks doing their own cooking and finding a place to lay down, I thought it was an inhuman way to transport people. Yes they did not pay much, but the unsanitary condition was bad.

I was given a place with the crew of the ship and had nothing to complain about. It was a very interesting eight days for me. But could not close my eyes to the way these native people were treated. Even on board of the navy ship they were kept apart from the white crew, doing their own cooking which is in cases hard for us to understand. For example, they like fish but it must be almost stinking before using it.

We had at times live pigs on board to be butchered. Everything from the inside of the hog they gathered and all cut in small pieces and cooked in a pot, and with all kinds of peppers added to it. One would wonder what it would taste like. But the good meat of the pig they would not eat. Yet I could get along just fine, if you would show interest in them, and try to learn their language. Most of them were used to serve the officers in the mess hall, and for cleaning. Some were in the engine room, and most were low class sailors I had mostly to work with.

The purpose of this vessel was to lay mines, to shut off the bay, and every so often we practice this. One day string out those mines. Next day take them in again. These were very busy days for the whole crew.

Whenever we were laying for anchor in more or less shallow water, 30-40 feet, it was a real treat to watch all the beautiful fish swimming in that clear water, big and small and the most tropical colored fish you have seen. The water in some places so clear I could follow the anchor chain to the anchor, which is very seldom.

One day we set out on the boom a big fish hook attached to a one inch line. A pretty good size piece of meat on the hook hanging, just dangling in the water. All was quiet on board during noon hour. I was walking the deck watch. And all of a sudden an eighteen foot shark took the hook and the rope was running out fast, and belaying the rope, the hook did set in its mouth and was surely hooked. Everybody got with the commotion on deck, and the commander wanted to take that big fish on deck and this was a real experience to bring that big fish in. So strong, so wild, even after cutting the whole belly open, it was twitching that tail.

After opening the stomach to learn what its last meal has been. However, nothing was found, and after cutting the jaw to be boiled and to pull all the teeth for us as a proof we got a shark, the tail was cut and put on a flagpole, which is an old custom. It was also surprising how soon the native on shore knew we had a shark. They came in their dugout and they were only looking for the lungs and entrails. After everything was set overboard and all the blood was cleaned from deck, we could smell the stink a couple of weeks later. To me this whole thing was a rich experience .

In so many ways those tropical islands are so beautiful, so rich, so serene. Time difference of the days was only 20 minutes over the whole year. Twilight between night and day is only 15 minutes. At times I was sent out with three-four men to go to the shore where I was to get a couple of tubs of white sand to be used to scrub the deck. On one of those trips we were all of a sudden surrounded with a group of sword fish. They are flat, about eight-ten feet wide, have a long tail which can do a lot of harm when you are hit. I had no idea what was going on all around. They made a lot of disturbance and so close I really got concerned as they were swimming and diving under the boat. Getting on shore, we loaded the tubs with sand and got back to ship all excited and thankful for that new experience. I felt kind of sad leaving this ship after those eight months, wondering what lay ahead of me.

After arriving July 1920 at the airport for navy flying service, I began my flying career, which lasted twelve years. Although a navy man still, had from this time on nothing to do with ships anymore.

This navy flying service was as yet in its beginning, a half dozen pontoon planes was all there was. But we did quite a bit of flying to train ourselves in navigation gunnery. In fact, becoming an all around observer. However it did not take long for me to wish I could fly the ship myself, instead of sitting in the back of the plane. Yet it was very interesting and exciting and so much to learn. Of course, that we made five guilder an hour was kind of attractive too. It was always flying over water and the only communication with the base, in case we had trouble, was with carrier pigeons. It was all so primitive.

One thing I always will remember, when flying over the outlet of a river, there were a whole bunch of shark picking up everything edible that came floating down the river. Not much chance to survive.

When I put in a request to receive training for pilot it was a surprise to me to be sent back to Holland before my three year stint was served.

Those two and one half years in the Indies has also been a wonderful experience. There was much sickness and one must be careful what to drink or eat.

I arrived back in Holland July 1921, being on the boat just one month. I had a pleasant reunion with the family. In their eyes, I was the hero of the family. Arriving at the airport Kooi, at the navy base in the city of Den Helder, received our first flying lesson, which for some sad reasons was postponed for several months. First an instructor with a student got killed. Shortly after, two officers taking up a plane that had just been overhauled, being up in the air about 2000 feet,the covering of the top wing tore loose and not having parachutes at that time, lost their lives. Then on top of that an advanced student went beyond his ability and got killed. This was the beginning of my flying career. I did not lose my ambition, but surely, I became very conscious about the dangers involved.

After new instructors were appointed, I finally began training and shall I ever forget my first solo flight on Jan. 13, 1922. As I mentioned before, from the time I was a child I had developed a certain degree of faith in prayer and during my flying days, standing on the starting line I would never open the trottle or I would ask for protection over the things I had no control over, considering all the close calls all the unexpected events that usually comes to all of us. I have felt so often of that protecting care, which has strengthened my faith.

After receiving my flying licenses for land and water planes, I was appointed as instructor, which placed upon me greater responsibilities. It has been great satisfaction to see most of my students develop in first class navy pilots. Yet see one of my advanced students coming down and lose his life one will never forget.

As a young pilot not even allowed to fly with a mechanic but had a sack with sand as ballast, was sent on my first cross country solo flight. As my course led me over the neighborhood I was born I could not resist to go to lower altitude and to show off my ability to fly an airplane. My folks and neighbors running out of their houses and I waving to them to let them know it was me. Making turns and some wing overs showing off and satisfying my vanity and pride. All this was strict against the rules. Going back to the base. I begin to worry what would happen if this was reported. Yes sir, a couple of days later I was called (what we used to call) to come on the carpet.

The commander of the airport showed me a piece out of the local papers where in an article of my showing off was greatly exaggerated by the reporter of that paper. Here I stood trembling of fear that I would be kicked out. And I guess seeing the fear on my face, he gave me a strong reprimand and I did thank the Lord that I got off this way. It was kind of natural seeing so few planes flying at that time that a reporter would find the occasion to write such a glorious article welcome more so he knowing my folks and mention their names.

During the years as a navy pilot trained as a fighting pilot, we had in those days single seater fighting planes, at that time the famous Fokker D7. It was a nice plane to make all kinds of stunts, and among us pilots, there was a great deal of rivalry going on, who could do the most daring stunts. I loved this stunting and anything you love to do you will learn well.

On my very last day in the navy, I had made up my mind to give the people of the airport, my fellow flyers, a number of air acrobatics they would long remember. After dinner I got the best plane which had a stronger motor on the line all set to show off and to satisfy my vanity and pride. As I was putting on my flying clothing a very heavy fog rolled over the field which kept me from taking off. This was not so unusual at that part of the country, usually it would clear up again in a short while.

I became more and more impatient, the fog did not lift until it was time to close up and the sky was perfectly clear again. When I came to my senses, I began to see the hand of the Lord, and felt so grateful to the Lord as he had seen fit to send that fog over the field, which kept me from taking any kind of risk in satisfying my pride and vanity. And asking to be forgiven and be mindful in the future. After saying farewell to all my friends, some of them would be loosing their lives in the 10 years later. After 17 years coming back I found a big pile of rubble completely destroyed during the second world war.

This is the end of my navy career - March 1930.

Flying in America

I will now continue writing about my flying experience after coming to this country. After being engaged for almost ten years as a military pilot, now I was to get to work myself in the commercial end of this business. Now it was the question to make money. This was quite a change for me, and being used to fly with the most up to date planes at that time, I was now flying those old slow planes for a small company. This high altitude and this mountain country was something I had to get used too. Yet it was for me exciting. Away from all those military rules and regulations, I felt so unspeakably free, coming to this great country.

Finding my way, learning the language, and trying to make a living took all my thoughts, even so much I was almost forgetting I had a wife and two boys. I was spending so much time at the airport. The whole purpose of coming to this country was for the sake of the gospel, to be with the people of the church we had joined. Here over I will write much more. Anyway, here it was where I failed. Neglecting the church by working seven days a week just to make a few dollars.

I met a man, Harry Gray was his name, who had a plane, but could not fly passengers. He made a deal to let me fly his plane and taking up passengers. I made 25 percent. Whenever somewhere a celebration was going on I would take the plane and try to find a suitable strip to land, was ready to do business. This was always a risky business flying over town a few rounds trying to get the people to come to the landing place, sometimes we made good, other times it was a failure. Yet the experiences I got was worth something. This kind of flying was called barnstorming. And as I was in it with all my heart, I did not see the risk involved too much.

During the two and one half years I was flying for this man and for the Thompson flying service, I have felt the Lords protecting care a number of times.

It was on a trip to Reno, where I was taking two men. Coming back from Reno, I needed to land in Elko to take some fuel. After gasing up it was dark but I wanted to go back to Salt Lake. Standing on the starting lines I had a distinct feeling to stay overnight. Next morning starting up the motor all was OK. Just after I was airborne the motor failed cold, and by quick maneuvering, I just got to a stop at the end of the field. This I never could have done in the dark. It pays to listen to these promptings.

One day we took the plane to Roosevelt, Utah, where the Indians had a big celebration once a year. This promised to be a big day. As I landed in a long alfalfa field. I could not see the land being corrugated, broke a strut off the landing gear. Here we were 140 miles from home hoping to make a good day. All we could do was to cut wire from a fence and wrap it around as good as possible and finding a smooth place to take off for home.

On the way back we had the closest call to get in serious trouble. Parleys Canyon was weather closed, turned back to Provo Canyon and decided that I could make it. The further I got in the lower the clouds. Never had a chance to turn back, had to go no matter the risk. On the end of the canyon is located the Provo power house and bearly missing the power lines. I found my way over the tree tops to the railroad going through the Jordan narrows and found the way to the airport. I had the owner and his wife with me on this trip. But they did not dare to look outside the plane as they told me later on. There I flew that many hours, had all the risk and made not a penny.

On a trip to Preston, Idaho, we had a wonderful day. I took in $300, made $90. We could live off that for a month as cheap as things were at that time.

On a trip to Logan, Utah, I landed on a piece of land that looked good from the air, but coming down in a wet spot the plane stood on its nose, pulling down the tail, we inspected the propeller. Yes we found a crack close to the hub, what now? I decided to take the plane up for a few rounds and see if the crack got any bigger. Flew all day taking passengers, and turned back to Salt Lake after dark, landing there in the dark without having lights on the plane. Rules were not very strict at that time.

The depression was getting worse. Banks were in trouble. Flying for Thompson I got a job to take two federal officers with half a million dollars to Boise, Idaho to save the bank. They were heavily armed in case I was making a forced landing, to protect the money. On my way back I was alone and coming to the airfield of the army, at Mountain Home, a spark plug blew out. All I needed to do, stop the motor and made a deadstick landing. The mechanic found a plug and I was on my way within a half hour. This could have easily happen over the most hazardous country. But my guardian angel was there to protect me. Oh how I appreciate this faith promoting experience.

One day we took the plane to Tooele. Finding a good strip of ground close to town, we made a deal with the community to take for a 7-8 minute ride all people over 65. I took up 45 elderly people over 65 plus all the younger ones. Also took up a parachute jumper. This fellow was plenty nervous, and I sure was glad when he left the plane. This was 24th of July celebration.

One day two elderly ladies wanted a ride, mother and daughter. Mother had her 80 birthday and this was a present. I had to promise not to do any stunts which I gladly did. It was a pleasure for me to see the joy she had of her first airplane ride.

Flying for Thompson, about three o'clock a lady came down to be taken to Los Angeles. She has missed her plane to the coast. We had a plane like the one Lindberg flew over the ocean in 1927. Yes I was taking her, but never been there. I felt it was quite a job. All I had was a regular road map, a flashlight, and one flare in case I had to make a force landing. Since that time I have never been able to understand how that man could have flown that plane with extra gas tank loaded to capacity for 33 hours. This lady had quite a lot of luggage, was smoking one cigarette after the other, asking all kinds of questions, while I needed all my attention to stay on the track.

Landing in Las Vegas to fill up and taking off again when dark. It was a beautiful full moon and flying from light upon light. I finally got through San Bernidino Pass. I was getting plenty tired, coming out of the pass, I saw nothing but light, light, light, and nothing but light wherever I looked. Had no clear idea where Burbank airport was, only the general direction.

I kept tracing the map with a flashlight. Then seeing a runway and deciding it would be the right one, I prayed earnestly to be guided to the right airport. I kept on going not knowing what I was doing except keeping the plane in the air. Then I saw some cross runways and felt this must be Burbank, even if it was not, would have landed anyway. Making a perfect landing, oh how thankful I felt of my prayer being answered. Taxing to the building, her husband was there to greet her. She gave five and he gave me $10, this was a royal tip in those days. After getting the luggage out, I found a motel room and being exhausted, I slept til nine.

Next morning after a nice shower, took off for Las Vegas. Climbing above the Los Angelos smog, which is at the time like a thick fog. Had a very nice trip home. Thankful for the wonderful experience. Also thankful to know I could rely on in time of need.

My most treasured experience I ever got has been on a day I was sent out with a small plane (pusser type) to assist some cowboys in the desert between Green River, Utah and Hanksville, rounding up wild horses. It was a very nice day. This plane has only a 25 HP motor, carried only 8 gallon gas, landing around Spanish Fork to take some gas. Climb to 10,000 feet going in a straight course to the desert, which led me about 20-25 mile south of Soldier Summit.

Being about cross of the summit, a voice just as clear as can be said Keep the highway. It was not a loud voice but so clear. This made me look around and did not comprehend, but I knew I was alone and my knowledge of distance, airspeed, and gas comsumption made me keep my course. The second time again that voice more pressing said Keep the highway. I got more confused, keeping the course, for the third time still more pressing said Keep the highway.

Disregarding all my arguments, I changed my course to the highway, coming out right above the summit, that 25 HP motor stopped with a bang. Setting the plane down along the highway, 200 feet from a telephone. While I was changing my course all feeling of anxiety left me and I felt at ease. (While I was doing something against my better knowledge.) Calling the airport, they came down with a flatbed truck and before dark we were home. Next morning, with a different plane took care of the job.

During the time I was waiting for the truck, I had time when I came to my senses, to see the hand of the Lord. After figuring out on the map where I would have been if I had not followed the voice, I would have been above the most hazardous country one can think of. Of all the force landing I have made, I always was able to reach a runway. Always has prayed for protection over things I had no control over.

How grateful I am for this marvelous experience. Now I knew for myself for sure that voices from on high or from the unknown can communicate and we can have a guardian angel to protect and watch over us. And as I have prayerfully asked for protection I never could have received a clearer answer. This force landing being the only landing I made out side a field in all my flying days. This has strengthened my testimony and my appreciation for the teaching of the church and for the gospel.

On this Submarine I served 2½ Jear. Had in 1918 an experience with gave me a Promotion to Boatsman mate as a reward. For bringing back the boat when it was adrift

[On this submarine I served 2 and one half year. Had in 1918 and experience wich gave me a Promotion to Boatsman mate as a reward. For bringing hack the boat when it was adrift.]

Landvliegtuig De Kooy den Helder

1926
This was one of the advanged plane. 350 HP motor wich was at that time a big Power plant those Hargars made of lumber were destroyd. May 5 1940

[This was 1926 one of the advanced plane 350HP motor wich was at that trime a big Power plant. those Hargars made of lumber were desroyed May 5 1940]

Watervliegtuig W 55.

On this type of seaplane I started out as a observer in 1920 in the Indies

[On this type of seaplane I started out as a observer in 1920 in the Indies]

This plane I made my solo Flight with in 1925 on the airdrome De Mok on the island of Texel N° Holl

[This plane I made my solo flight with in 1925 on the airdrome De Mok on the island of Texel, No. Holl]

[Picking up the torpedo shot from the sub]

Picking up the torpedo, shot from the sub

PHOTOS OF DESCRIPTIONS Give names, addresses if possible, and how connected to you. *(Neighbor, school friend, etc.)*

THREE PARACHUTE JUMPS FEATURE AIR EXHIBITION

summer of 1930

More than 10,000 air-minded fans gathered Sunday afternoon to witness the "air circus" at the municipal airport which was sponsored by commercial flying organizations.

As a feature of the afternoon, three parachute jumps were made by Sig Smith, famed daredevil and hero of many breathtaking feats. It had been previously planned that his wife, Babe Smith, who usually co-stars with him in these parachute jumps, would also make some jumps, but the swiftness of the wind made jumping seem to dangerous and she didn't attempt it. Likewise, the original plan of giving a glider demonstration had to be abandoned.

Pilots of the planes from which the jumps were made were John Campbell, H. Dinkelman and Lewis Conner. Smith used a 32-foot parachute in making his jumps.

A series of flying stunts which included loop-the-loops, barrel-rolls, wing-overs and tailspins were staged by Campbell and Dinkelman.

Tentative plans are being made now to put on another air circus on Memorial day, May 30, it was announced Sunday.

Bill Stoven with the great lakes

HILVERSUM, 20 April 1923.

Een stout vliegenier.

— Gedurende de laatste dagen wordt onze gemeente bezocht door een vliegenier, die in zeer hooge regionen proeven van bekwaamheid op luchtvaartgebied aflegt en daardoor zeer de belangstelling trekt van het publiek. Soms beschrijft hij hoog in de lucht groote cirkels om plotseling in een fraaie glijvlucht zeer laag te dalen, zoodat het publiek denkt dat de aviateur een noodlanding maakt en men zich spoedt in de richting van den Laarderweg waarboven de vlieger langen tijd heeft gemanoeuvreerd. Van een noodlanding is echter geen sprake, want eensklaps ziet men de machine zeer hoog weer in de zon schitteren om spoedig opnieuw als een pijl uit den boog naar beneden te schieten zoodat de menschen vol angst den reusachtigen vogel langs de daken over het spoor zien scheren. Na eenigen tijd zijn vaardigheid in de vliegkunst te hebben vertoond, vliegt de koene aviateur naar Soesterberg terug. Dat hij juist boven onze gemeente zijn stoute kunsten komt vertoonen, vindt zijn oorzaak hierin, dat deze vlieger een Hilversummer is, de zoon van de familie D. in de Bakkerstraat. Daarom demonstreert hij boven de Spoorwijk en vliegt hij zoo laag mogelijk boven het ouderlijke huis om zijn familie de proeven van zijn bekwaamheid te kunnen toonen.

A free translation of the [illegible] flyer
During the last few days this community has been visited
by a flyer who in high altitude gave evidence of
his skill as a airman, and very much drew the attention
of the public. After flying high, than in a daring dive flys
low of the homes, making the public belief of having to
make a force landing. Than again climbing high and
again as a arrow comes down, After a few more daring
stunts the daring flyer return to his base.
The reason he comes this way to show his ability.
He is born in this town and is a son of the family
Dinkelman in the Bakkerstraat.
That reporter sure gave me more credit than
I had coming, [illegible] [illegible] lost my chance to become
a aviator on account of this [illegible].

[Article about showoff flying over home town]

I was not even far enough in training to take a macanic with me.

showing of and inspection during Queens birthday
This are the at time the famous Fokker D-VII.

This History Is Mine

This plane I flew to L Angles
story on page 25
same Lindabug flew
the ocean 1927

Mine Instructor

Some of mine Students

1923 my Pride possesion

Flying along the Graff zeppelin

Flat tire

This has folding wing to be taken on
board of a ship.

Jacoba Wachter Dinkelman

Family of Origin and Personal History

Born November 21, 1903, in Den Helder, Netherland
Married to Hendrik Dinkelman, December 12, 1923 in Rotterdam, Holland
Children: Jan Hendrik, Willem Adriaan
Father: Wilhelm Adriaan Wachter
Mother: Petronella Bruin

My twin brother and I were born one month prematurely, and my twin brother died when he was two and one half years old. My parents had seven children altogether, four girls and three boys. [Johan Conrad 1899-1899, Jacoba 1901-1901, Wilhelm Adriaan 1902-1975, Hermus Martinus 1903-1905, Jacoba 1903-1998, Helena Antje 1908-2002] My father was a Protestant and my mother a Catholic but all of us children were raised in the faith of our mother.

My father was a career man in the Dutch Navy and served as a Ship's Boatsman and Maintenance Officer. During his navy career, he was stationed in the Dutch East Indies twice for four years altogether where he was responsible for the upkeep of the naval ship he served on.

After he retired from the Navy, he moved to Rotterdam, Holland, where he became the manager, designer and maintenance man of a German Row and Sailboat Association. He also owned and operated the bar there, but when mother became ill and I got married, he sold out and bought a home in the country in Apeldoorn, Holland, where he and my mother retired.

I went to grade school and after graduating from there, I went to Home Economics School where I took sewing courses. I never used it as a profession, but only for my own and my family's benefit. After I finished school, I stayed home to help my mother with household chores.

During my younger years, I also learned to dance, swim and play the piano, but I will never forget what a tomboy I was when I was a little girl. My parents were quite well to do and my mother always dressed me in pretty clothes and boots or shoes, but I loved to climb trees and walk through the mud with my pretty boots and in the rain when I wore pretty clothes and velvet caps.

I was quite a rascal in school also and must have given my teachers a real bad time by playing instead of learning and was therefore often punished by having to stay after school was out.

While living in Rotterdam with my parents, I occasionally went to visit my aunt who lived in Den Helder. On one of these visits, I met a young navy man named Henk who stayed in her house as a boarder. We became very interested in each other but I really fell In love with his motorcycle first before I fell in love with him. We became engaged which led to our marriage on December 12, 1923.

When we married, my husband , was a Protestant, promised my mother that our children would be raised as Catholics. Although I had been born and raised as a Catholic, after my marriage and when our first son Jan was born, for some unknown reason I did not want our son to be baptized a Catholic and neither did my husband. This was a great tragedy for my mother who was a very devout Catholic woman. I felt that the children who would be born unto us should be free to choose their own religion. My husband and I both prayed about the matter and when the Mormon Missionaries came into our lives and taught us about the Gospel and baptism for children, I knew then that it was right for babies to be blessed only, and to be baptized when they were old enough to be able to understand the difference between right and wrong.

On September 1, 1927, we were baptized in the North Sea. We applied for immigration to America and although my husband was a navy career man and we had a good life and everything we wanted, he gave it all up to bring us to Zion.

We left Rotterdam by boat on March 23, 1930. On our way to Salt Lake City, we stayed over in Denver, Colorado for three days to meet my husband's aunt and uncle who lived there. They were religious and active people in their own church and very much opposed to the Mormon Church, but treated us well during our stay with them.

After our arrival in Salt Lake City on April 6, 1930, we first rented a house but about eight months later, we were able to buy a little home of our own. In 1933, we traded this home in for a 27 acre farm in Granger. This was a big undertaking in our lives and we experienced real hardship during the first three years. We didn't know a single thing about farming or animals and my husband had to learn to do real manual labor. With the help of our good neighbors, however, he learned how to milk our 6 cows, how to put harnesses on our 3 horses and how to plant crops. He worked very hard and drove himself to the limit. I baked a lot of bread and we had enough to eat from the farm but we had no cash money to buy anything else because all the money and savings we had was invested in the farm.

Although these first three years were difficult ones, especially when our finest cow and her new born calf died and one of our few horses got trapped in a ditch and died, we also learned to appreciate the few things we did have. It was a thrill to see grain coming up out of the ground, how grateful we were for rain when it was badly needed and how thankful we were when a litter of pigs or a calf was born.

Now, remembering and looking back on our mishaps and failures, I realize that they have been blessings in disguise as when I was in the hospital when my husband, with his last savings, bought chickens and a chicken coop which blew over during a big dust storm. This happening made us appreciate the Elders of the Ward who came together to put the chicken coop up again.

As a family, we were happy going on canyon outings, taking homemade cake and lemonade along, until we had to trade in our car for an old truck and a cow. When the truck wouldn't run and the cow died, we just had to start all over again.

Our boys thought that their best time was spent helping at the farm, even if the work was hard. When we were about to lose the farm, we were able to get a loan to help us along. My husband started working at Kennecot Copper to earn cash money but with the help of our sons, he kept the farm going and began to raise better crops. After I had managed to save $450.00, I bought my husband a tractor so he could get rid of the team of horses we had. One was lazy and the other one was absolutely crazy.

Now the farm work could be done in much less time and even I could run it with the help of the boys while my husband worked for Kennecot Copper Corporation.

After World War II had started in 1941, there was a great need for men and women to work in the ammunition factories. In 1942, I got a job in a small arms plant in North Salt Lake where I worked night shift soldering bullet-proof boxes to be send overseas. I did this for 13 months until the plant closed. With the money I earned, we were able to pay off the farm.

When our oldest son Jan went to war, keeping the farm became too much. We sold it and bought a house on 3775 South and 7th East. We liked the house but it needed a lot of repairs in and outside. However, my husband found pleasure in fixing and improving our home.

In 1947, my husband was called on a Mission to the Netherlands. With our son Jan in the Service stationed in Japan, our son Bill in the Coast Guard in Portland *[Maine]* and my husband in the Netherlands, I became lonely and restless. I made arrangements with two school teachers to rent our house and six months after my husband had left, I followed him to Holland.

I only planned to visit him while he was there but Mission President Zappy called me on a Mission while I was there and for 18 morths I was happy to be able to labor with my husband as a Missionary. The two school teachers had paid for 18 months rent in advance and I used that money to pay for my mission expenses.

After our return to Salt Lake City on April 6, 1949, our sons home again but before too long, both got married. Our house now became a little too big for just the two of us and my husband decided to sell it and bought a smaller house between Main and State Street about 3100 South - Miller Avenue.

Then an old friend of ours, who was in fact the first missionary *[Ray Hutchinson]* who had knocked on our door, told us of an old gentleman who had suffered a stroke which had left him helpless. He had also lost his wife and needed a couple to take care of him. This man turned out to be the Bishop of the first ward we lived in some 27 years ago and who had been so very helpful to us. We felt great compassion for him since he wanted so much to stay in his own home and be taken care - and it looked as if he would not live for more than a few weeks – we closed our own home to temporarily move into his house to take care of him. He lived for seven more months before he passed away. When we were then offered to buy his home, we sold our own home and moved in to his place which was in a much nicer neighborhood at 2002 East 21st South.

After living there for six years, we sold that house and bought a home at 7150 South 9th East that had a big chicken coop on the property. We intended to plant fruit trees and after my husband tired, to go into the chicken business. Instead, he was called upon to become a Temple Worker. Because he did not like traveling that far to the Temple so early in the morning and also because I had to stay home alone with no transportation available, we sold our home again and this time rented an apartment close to the Temple where we still live.

The Lord has been good to me and my family. Right after World II broke out in May 1940 in Holland, my one year older brother Wim (Bill), who was an "Adelborst" (Naval Cadet) was immediately assigned along with several other Naval Cadets to take Queen Wilhelmina of the Netherlands to England by boat. They survived severe bombardment while crossing the North Sea and the Strait of Dover and my brother remained in England until the war was over. My brother's wife was totally unaware of the event until she was informed by other Naval Cadets of the successful escape of the Queen which had involved the help of her husband. She did not see him again until the war ended in May 1945.

My oldest brother Johan was taken prisoner by the Germans during the war. All able German men, young and old, had been drafted into the Service. Although some factories closely located near concentration camps were able to get Jewish prisoners as laborers, Germany was in desperate need of more labor help to keep its factories going. Many Gentile men were therefore taken away from their homes and families to be transported to Germany where they became prisoners doing labor work. My brother managed to escape by jumping from the train and went back home. He was not bothered again by the Germans during the rest of the war. Most of these Gentile men were free to go home again after the war had ended, but some were never heard of again.

The Lord has also greatly blessed my husband and me in that both our sons were married in the Temple. Our oldest son Jan was assigned to a tank division in World War II and was a survivor of the Invasion of Normandie. He now is a Warrant Officer in the Army-Sea Transportation Corps and is presently stationed in Virginia. He is married to Alice DiDonato and they have one girl and two boys, one of whom has served on a Mission in New Zealand.

Willem (Bill) served in the Coast Guard, worked at some professional and non-professional jobs and decided to settle down in East Carbon County and work in the coal mine. He is first counselor in the Bishopric in his ward and is married to Ottoline *[Ottalyne]* Hansen. They have two girls and three boys, one of whom has been on a combined French-Swiss Mission.

I am indeed grateful for my good husband, who is a High Priest in the 17th Ward, Salt Lake Stake, and for our children, grandchildren and the five great-grandchildren we have to date. I am thankful to be a member of the Church for I know that it is the true Church of Jesus Christ of Latter-Day Saints.

The Wachter Family

circa 1907
Father: Wilhelm Adriaan Wachter (in back)
Mother: Petronella Bruin
children:
John Conrad, Jacoba, Helena Antje, Wilhelm Adriaan

"Wim" [Wilhelm], Jacoba and Helena Antje
Wachter
circa 1913 Holland

from back of photo
"Wilem and Petronella wachter with grandson
John Dinkelman
circa 1926"

Jacoba and twin Hermanus Martinus
Wachter
[Hermanus passed away at 18 mos of age]

Petronella and Wilhelm Wachter

Johan Conrad 1930's

Wilhelm Adriaan 1930's

John Wachter   Jacoba Dinkelman   Wilhelm Wachter   Hendrik Dinkelman
November 1948
Amsterdam Holland

Johan Wachter   Wilhelm Wachter

"Vader en Moeder Wachter"
unknown grandchild

Helena Antje (Lena) Willem Adriaan (Wim) Petronella Bruin Willem Adriaan
"Toet" (wife of Wim) "Born in East Indies"
[info from the back of photo]
10 August 1930

Wim's family-- notable center row seated
Wim- light suit Father Wacther Mother Wacther
GAANJE DEEGE - only photo of W. Wachter's sister
[info from back of photo]

Jacoba at Ray Hutchinson's dairy farm in
Heber Utah

est. 10 years of age

circa. 1920's

Jacoba thru the years

1947 Portland Oregon

Late 1940's Mission photo

1950's

early 1970's

1985

Our Marriage and Conversion

12 Dec 1923

As a boatwain mate, well established in my work and about 25 years of age, had the natural desire to get my own little place to live, and to have more privacy to do study. I rented a room plus a stalling place for my motorcycle by an elderly widow.

One day, one daughter of this widow's sister came to visit her, getting kind of interested with this young girl, invited her for a ride on the motorcycle. She had not been away from her home very much. Taking her for a longer ride than I should have done, her aunt was plenty worried that something would have happen to that young girl. She has been married to a navy man and know something of those sailor boys. However, there was no danger for that girl.

This motorbike ride was the beginning of a courtship, which was way too short to become well acquainted. But she living with her parents in another city, and I only could visit her on weekends, once in three weeks. It was not ideal for both of us and I believe on that account, we got married sooner as was good for us. She being 19 years old, but inexperienced as she was and I being on my own feet since I was 14. I had no brains enough to call for mature counsel. I made one mistake after the other. I was knowing it all, and I thought she was too young to know anything. How dumb can a man be!

Of course, when this came up, questions arose. She being raised in the Catholic faith, and I being a Protestant, brought all kinds of warnings and kinds of troubles, which would surely prevent the marriage to last not even a year. This marriage outside ones faith was always looked upon to be risky.

I was not a church goer, but I had much faith in sincere prayer. And prayed often what I should do. With all these warning, I really needed to know. However, her father, also a navy man, was of the Protestant faith, and it was a good marriage, which did help me to make the decision to go ahead. Her mother asking me if I would be willing to have the future children to be raised in the Catholic faith, made me promise to have them baptized in the Catholic church. Her mother being a devout Catholic, this did mean so much to her. And as far as I could know, I too (just like her husband) would be compelled to leave home for a tour of duty for three years and the bringing up would be left to the mother.

So we were married 12 Dec. 1923 in the city of Rotterdam. The beginning of much needed adjustment in this man's way of thinking. Use to living his own way, making his own decisions, so much independent and so entirely giving my thoughts to my flying responsibilities as an instructor, almost put my young wife in the second place. Which altogether made our start in marriage life less satisfying and falling short of our ideals. It even was sometimes said "he is more in love with his flying job as with his wife." After being married 60 years at the time of this writing, how wonderful it would be to be able to set the clock back. And knowing what I know now and do it over again. I just had no sense to know that after much learning, our ideals can become a reality. Learning to be patient, learning self control or rather the lack of these things brought loss of self respect, strife and misunderstanding, and a feeling of failure. Yet I always have felt she being the one for me, and after all these years I must give her all the credit for whatever success we have had, for her faithfulness and willingness to endure.

Becoming pregnant so soon was not what we expected or really wanted. Wishing we could have some time to getting to knowing each other and to enjoy each other during those months carrying our first child. Oh how much we were in need of wise counsel and communication with older people, but living away from parents we were left to ourselves. And by the way, this man was too self centered to seek that counsel. But when the time came for our son to be born, very soon I had to make good my promise to have him baptized in the Catholic church. I did not know why but somehow we just could not do it, and as I made this promise in good faith, it became a pressing issue for me. It made me feel like a heel.

With all my short comings, I still was seeking help in prayer. This question of baptizing our son was lingering on for better than two years. And realizing the concern of our parents and especially the grieve my mother-in-law was suffering for me not keeping my promise. As according to the Catholic faith, if something would happen to that boy, he absolutely would be a lost soul and hell would be his destination. This was, with the other unpleasant conditions, bearing down on both of us and not knowing what to do, only it was decided if not in the Catholic then also not in the Protestant church. Yet somehow I felt that an answer would come, and my prayer would be answered. It is easy to realize the feeling that existed in the family, not that this ever came out in the open, but it sure was there. Looking back, I have always felt that lack of communication is the devils tool of 95 percent of all the disharmony and breaking up relationship within families.

Of course, we did not know, but the Lord has laid out his plan. At about 1926 the Lord sent to our home two young missionaries [*Elder Albert Venema and Elder Ray Hutchinson*] and being impressed, after being invited, with their humility and sincerity, we felt confident to ask questions, which they were able to answer from the scripture. The question of baptism was foremost on our mind, and after we were made acquainted, met the writings of Moroni pertaining to baptism for children, all our burden was lifted from us and all feeling of guilt was taken from me. Yes, we had to wait more than two years for an answer, but it was clear to us. This had been the start of an entirely different direction of our lives.

The teachings of the restored gospel has given direction in all our undertakings, gradually changing our whole way of living. Of course, it did not come all at once, but to the degree I gained knowledge of the restored gospel and learned to apply that knowledge in our daily lives, we made progress. Slow but sure. From the start of our marriage, full with the highest ideals which were impossible to attain brought discouragement and disappointment because we, inexperienced as we were, needed to learn to control our emotions, learn to be humble and more willing to forget ourselves for the sake of the good of another, more trust in the Lord and be patient in waiting for the Lord's answers. This accepting the gospel and, in due time becoming a member of the Mormon church we never heard of before, brought all kinds of questions and all kinds of revelations, in fact an altogether new insight of the meaning of life. I was going, without knowing it, through the process of that what is so beautifully explained in the 32nd chapter of Alma. It all became sweet to me.

I will always be thankful for the missionaries in giving me the desire to learn more and to try to live that I had learned to be true. Here I was at the time of life when I had the idea I knew all there is to know. Being successful in my occupation, making good money, having my own home and independent, thought I had the world by the tail. There come two young well dressed fellows handing us some pamphlets to read, telling us it was a message of great value. First impression was, they were just one of the many religions that was going around the country and just laid those pamphlets aside. But persistently coming back each week and the way they presented themselves made us aware they had a message. I have never read anything about the Mormon church, and now as we were going to investigate, all kinds of articles and even a book came my way telling us how terrible the teachings of that church was, some even so bad, it could not be believed. Perhaps it was a good thing that those anti-Mormon literature was so bad as it did not keep me from investigating their message. How more the light of the gospel came upon us, how more we knew this literature to be the work of Satan and it never had any influence upon me anymore.

Now don't get the idea that I all of a sudden became a faithful and active member of the church, and did not have my doubts about certain subjects. Yet certain conditions in our married life were crying for something to happen, which by the way of these two boys brought to pass this great change of direction in our future life. From then on our marriage and our conversion did run together.

Normally, I would have stayed in the navy, would have advanced two more promotions and would, by the age 50, retire with a substantial pension in 1948. However, I would have gone through the second world war. And in as much as so many fellows of my time serving in the flying service were killed, it is once questioned how I would have come out.

This then has been the beginning of a changed outlook upon life, a change that has led and directed us to this day. A change we are grateful for, as it has opened up new horizons, unlimited knowledge of the wonderful plan of the gospel and eternal life. Of course, man must learn the laws and principles of the gospel and to learn to obey them in order to gain that knowledge which can take us to a higher plane of understanding of the purpose of life here upon the earth. This hunger for more truth makes man forget his worldly troubles. Right from the start I felt the message they taught us was true, I had no doubt about this and being led to read and to ponder the words of Alma which are within the 32 chapter.

"But behold, if ye will awake and arouse your faculties even to experiment upon my words and exercise a particle of faith, yea, even if ye can no more than desire to believe in a manner that you can give place for a portion of my words. Now, we will compare the word unto a seed. Now if you give place, that a seed may be planted in your heart, behold if it is a good seed or a true seed, if you do not cast it out by your unbelief, that you will resist the Spirit of the Lord, behold it will begin to swell within your breasts; and when you feel these swelling motions, ye will begin to say within yourselves - It must needs be that this is a good seed, or that the word is good, for it beginneth to enlarge my soul; yea it beginneth to enlighten my understanding, yea it beginneth to be delicious to me."

Experience this in your own heart and mind. It has helped me so much to read and study scripture and increase my desire to come to a greater understanding of the marvelous plan of God pertaining to his children here on earth.

When I serious began to investigate and heard the story of the boy Joseph Smith in the grove, the appearances of the Father and the Son, the angel Moroni, Peter, James, John, and John the Baptist, it was all a mystery to me. Yet I did not reject these so far reaching events. But I told myself if these things are true, some day I will know for sure that they are true, and I will have faith and a testimony and will testify like so many has done in the past.

In our feeble start, we had to learn of the power of the adversary who would like nothing more than to destroy and frustrate our seeking for truth by bringing in my reach many anti literature I already wrote about.

Of course, I had my doubts and misunderstandings which always comes forth from my lack of understanding. The statement was made that a healthy doubt is good, if it makes us put up a greater effort to study and to pray. As I began to read the scripture more prayerful, my interest in the teaching of the church increased and the way the church has come forth through all the tribulation helped to clear up the mysteries. However, as we slowly were gaining knowledge we also became aware, that to learn the truth doesn't mean to practice the truth and to apply it in our daily life. Learning about the law of tithing and the Word of Wisdom or any other law is one thing, but to make it a part of your life is something else. I began to realize the great changes that must take place within me, the many things I needed to repent of. And I must admit the encouragement I received from my wife and many others. She being faithful even in the most trying circumstances. Instinctively, she felt that if our marriage was to be saved, it would be through the gospel This process of conversion has been a slow process but a steady one.

I didn't take long to realize how soon one can gain scriptural knowledge through reading, pondering and study, and awake to the fact that in practical living we stay far behind. And I have felt it is better to learn a certain principle and make it a part of your life than to gain a great deal of knowledge and struggle for many years to put them in practice. It has been my experience in connection with the use of tobacco. As long as I was struggling with obeying the Word of Wisdom there was not the spiritual progress. It said so plainly, bring forth fruits of repentance before one is ready for baptism, which was not in my case. It was so difficult for me to give up, and yet I tried so hard. While other principles were so easy for me to obey. Yet the struggle with the cigarette kept me from making progress as I could have made, this struggle is to be a story in itself.

It was at that time difficult for me to see, why it was so important to quit smoking, all the menfolk in the family were using tobacco, I have smelled smoke all my early youth. That it was not good for the body we never heard of, until I learn about the Word of Wisdom. I happened to be very much enslaved to it, something one only find out when you want to stop using it. But when I learn that it is the will of the Lord and began to believe that it was for my own good and I from now on was breaking the law of health knowingly. I had to learn that the first law of heaven is the law of obedience. When I got that far, I thought there was nothing to it. Taking a pack from the pocket and throwing it away. I found myself coming back to the spot and found it again. To make this quitting more easy, I bought $10 anti-smoke pills. Then after eating myself sick on those pills, I smoked that much more. This failing each time brought frustration, even to the point I did not care jitany more. But feeling unhappy, started all over again.

Bull headed, I was, without any help going to quit this habit, even if it was the last thing I was going to do. As long as I was not yet baptized I could not feel bound. But after I was baptized it would be a different matter. I learn that there is no progress but a feeling of unworthiness take hold, and loosing self respect. I also became aware, even a man can gain a testimony of the gospel and know the church being the true church, yet unless he learn to obey the law and the principles of the gospel, he can not receive the blessings there from. Even the devil know this is true.

Yes, I was showing myself that I could do it and on the night we left Rotterdam, I took every cigarette in my possession and threw them overboard. This was going to be the end. We were now on our way to Zion. Yet by four o'clock the little store on board ship opened up and I bought my first pack of Chesterfield, and completely disgusted with myself I gave up trying. How I needed someone to press me down on my knees and ask the Lord to bless me with the power to overcome. No sir, I had a better idea, I was not going to carry any cigarettes anymore. I was not being tempted anymore. But instead of losing a bad habit I was gaining a worse habit. I lowered myself by asking for a cigarette from anybody I thought who would give me one. This was too much. I then did not give a darn anymore, and kept even with a guilty feeling enjoying my smoke.

Now I know for sure the Lord knew all my struggle, and later on I have thought many times - where would I have been if it was not for the long suffering of the Lord.

Then one day my most treasured experience was going to happen. Leonard Harmon a faithful member who was 80% blind ask me to go with him home teaching. No sir, I am not worthy. "Come on, you will help me." More out of pitty I said "Okay, but don't you ask me to do anything." That was okay with him. The first home we went to was the elders quorum president and Bro. Harmon was this man's first counselor and they all knew of my habit and somehow I expressed my frustration about my weakness to overcome. Nothing was said but a few days later I was invited to a short meeting by the bishop and a few faithful brethren. I had no idea what was going to happen. About 12 priesthood holders were present. The bishop said "you have some trouble with the Word of Wisdom. We feel we can help you." As I became aware of what the purpose of the meeting was, the devil whispered in my ear "it can't be done, it can't be done." We all kneeled down and each in turn offered a word of prayer in my behave, the bishop being the last and said, "Henry you don't need to worry anymore." Again that whisper "it can't be done, it can't be done." My neighbor taking me home said, as I got out of the car, "All will be alright." And again "it can't be done, it can't be done."

Coming in the house it was getting late, my mind was not working right. Thinking about what has happen, I could not comprehend the significance of it. All of a sudden I pick up the half cigarette that lay on the stove and striking a match my hand was brought to a stop about six inches from my lips and down it went. Without any conscious thinking I again did strike a match and again my hand went down as at first. Not being aware of anything that was going on. I was, as it were, as a will less object standing between two great powers. I again for the third time, I took that cigarette in my mouth, again did strikes a match and again that unseen power kept my hand from lighting that cigarette even more forcibly taking my hand down. All this happen perhaps within 5 or 10 minutes. Yet I was not. really conscious of what was going on. Only I know this one glorious thing, that from that very hour I never had the least desire to have a smoke, even the smell of it was disagreeable to me. It took sometime for me to realize what had happened to me. And I can't find words to express my thanks to the Lord and those faithful priesthood holders.

A few days later, at fast meeting bearing my testimony, in my broken English, testifying of this marvelous manifestation of the spirit in my behalf brought many tears, especially to those men who were instrumental in this miracle. I had learned two important principles, first that a man can do very little without faith and can't trust in his own power. Second, now I knew that the power of the priesthood can be exercised in behalf of those who are in need of it. This great power, exercised in righteousness, will over rule the power of the adversary. I also testify that a man can be kept out of the church just by that little cigarette. I have heard many stories about heavy smokers all their lives, and also with least struggle lay their pipe, cigar or cigarette aside and quit. But perhaps the law of tithing or the law of fast or any other law of the gospel give them difficulties. The whole experience from start to finish has been a blessing to me.

The story of our immigration.

As I begin to write our story of our gathering to Zion, 54 years after us coming to this land of America, and by hind sight, realize all that has come forth out of it. We more clearly can see the hand of the Lord and the fulfilling his purposes, and how we have been guided step by step, and unknowingly, have been instruments in his hand.

When we on a regular basis began to investigate, I naturally became interested in this great land, and was asking many questions, more especially about the question of the gathering of the saint and all that has been written about it.

At that time (1930), not having built any temples in Europe, it was quite common among converts to get that spirit of gathering. So it was with us. Even before we were members of the church, a voice urged me to get a number on the immigration list, as only a certain number of people were allowed to enter in this country. This voice stayed with me until I went to the American Consul in Amsterdam and got my name on that list. As soon as I had done this I felt at ease, and that spirit of gathering got more or less in the background. Only we began to learn some English words. This time my flying career was the uppermost thing in my mind. The waiting time would be about three years and much could happen in that time.

The one bad thing I always will regret. We left our folks without any knowledge about our conversion and about our future plans until the time came we were ready to go. Several reasons led me to it. First, I was not far enough devout in the gospel in a way that it would mean anything to them. Second, I was too self-conscious, too proud to stand any of their ridicule of affiliating myself with a church of which they knew nothing but the most filthy things they heard of. Real communication was never a rewarding thing in either of the families. Yet Should have had courage regardless of what the reaction would have been.

It is because the sorrow it caused them seeing their daughter and the two little grandsons leaving them forever, as they thought, was very hard for them to bear. It was not possible for them to know what drove me. Here was a man with a successful navy career, having already 18 years of service with a promising future leaving his people, his native country, starting all over again in trying to establish himself, causing so much sorrow and grieve just for the sake of a belief in an unpopular church.

As time went on we began to think about this more and more. We started building up our savings account and try to learn a few English words. But should I really give up all those years of service? Give up my eligibility for a pension? Give up my flying career which I loved so much? Should I cause so much sorrow to our folks? We began wondering what we would do when time would come.

It was in the spring of 1927, I got my name on the list and now it was November 1929 and we began to learn about the financial troubles in the country. President Heber C. Grant being so well up to date with the financial condition found it wise to give counsel to those of the saints of different nations and who were contemplating of gathering to Zion to stay where they were for the time being. He could see the hardships that was waiting for them who even had, in many cases, to borrow the money for their fare. It just happen after reading his counsel in the the Star, we received the notice from the consul to decide to use our number or not. We made it a matter of prayer and the answer was there the next night.

The elders coming to our home to tell us that next Sunday Apostle Widstoe was coming to Amsterdam to visit Holland on a tour through the mission and wanted the elders to be there. To me, having much faith in the leaders of church, felt this was the answer to our prayers and decided to see him and to explain my situation. And made up my mind to listen and follow his counsel. After our situation was carefully explained to him by the elders, I will never forget, after he listen carefully and looked in my eyes and said, "Brother go." This "Brother go" from an apostle of Jesus Christ and having much faith all our obstacles were moved out of our way.

It is true that we had been able to build us a substantial savings account which allowed us to go without going in debt and did bring us safely through the worst part of the 1930-35 depression. Yes, we had to scrimp to the bare necessities and as we were placing our trust on our savings account, the Lord also saw fit to bring us to the last dollar and the lowest paid manual labor jobs, the very opposite of occupation I had before I left my native country. Yet it all made us more dependent on the Lord, which did work out for our own good. Now I testify I have never regretted of gathering to Zion. I testify a man can never go wrong in following the counsel of an apostle of the Lord.

Again, we could see the hand of the Lord, as we learn later that we were the next to last family who were allowed to enter the USA because immigration was brought to a stop for about five years. I realize that if I had not listen and had not followed up that voice of getting my number on the immigration list, we would have never come to this land, and would have been able to do all we have been able to do in these more than 50 years. Yes, we have been guided and directed in a very distinct way, even with all our weaknesses.

Making preparation to leave our native country and informing our people about our plans. It brought to pass a great deal of expressions of sorrow about us being led away to hell by this despicable church. Impossible for them to understand a man with such a great future and so successful could give it all up. Something must be wrong mentally. My father, who was a retired railroad man enjoying his pension, it was to him the ultimate of foolishness to give up that eligibility to my pension. For my father and my father-in-law, both enjoying their pensions, it was the most irresponsible thing for a man to do to give up his right to a deferred pension on account of going to another nation and accepting that citizenship. Of course, they were sincere in their judgement, but they did not know the ways of the Lord with all their sorrow and lamentations.

Yet none of them would take time to find out for themselves what motivated us to make this move, except getting information from ignorant or enemies of the Mormons. This was not a pleasant time. As I was not able to explain in a satisfying manner, to them the restored gospel, mainly on account of their prejudices. I quietly drew back rather than fall in unending arguments. There was none I could sit down with and tell about our conversion. And they were left in the dark for many years about our real reason of leaving.

Although I mention before: we were not making this move to get a better living. Only the spirit of gathering motivated us and were willing to sacrifice for it. Although we have never felt it to be such a sacrifice and have never felt sorry, only felt sorry for our folks, for them it was a mystery, for us because we could not make them understand.

The very last evening we spent with our folks, our son John five years old got with some little boys lost and being under pressure, as we were, running around until he was found. This was felt as an evil foreboding, as a sign we were doing the wrong thing.

Of course nobody could know that I and my little family ten years later would be spared to go through those five terrible years of the occupation which brought so much suffering to them.

Nobody could know that we, and mainly the wife, would be able to send some needed help as soon as it was allowed to sent 10 pound packages. She was able to gather so much clothing. We being the only ones in the position to do so and should have done much more as we have done.

Nobody could know that 28 years after we left, the law of the land pertaining to those who accepted citizenship in the USA, their eligibility to a deferred pension would be restored, just a year before I became 60 years old and at this writing enjoy this pension 23 years.

Nobody could know we would, after 17 years, come back on a two year mission and see one of their daughters and her family to join this church and are happy for doing so, and have been blessed according to their faithfulness. The wife and I being the first in our families to accept the gospel.

Nobody could know what would come forth out of our conversion, of the gathering of all the information about our ancestors, of all the work that has been done for them and their names are now found in the register of the temple.

Having been back four times and have had many occasions to testify of the restored gospel and a number of the family has had an opportunity to be taken on tours and see for themselves the outward accomplishments of the church, and make them acquainted with the teaching of the church, and notice the blessings that will come to those who will live according those teaching. Yet so far none has the desire nor the faith to follow and accept the principles as they are taught in this church.

We left 23 March 1930 with Holland American liner, New Rotterdam, very crowded with immigrants of different nations. However the weather was agreeable and we could spend much time on deck. It took nine days to arrive New York harbor, now it takes nine hours. Arriving at Hoboken, we were guided to the train by some fine people who made it their mission to render the help to those non-English speaking people. Which was very appreciated.

Passing that Statue of Liberty was an emotional event. And I would not know how to explain or express my feelings when coming up the habor of New York and seeing that statue. I was coming to start a whole new life and had the freedom to do so. This unbelievable feeling of freedom I have felt a number of times, which did help me so much to accept the challenge of starting a new life.

The train was not as clean as we expected, those coal burning engines gave a lot of dust. We had our son, John, five and one half, and our baby, 6 months, who were our greatest concern, to keep clean, and to give proper food. Three days and three nights is a long time in a mostly crowded train, and feeling so much the lack of being able to speak the language. I had informed my aunt in Denver that we were coming to the USA and were invited to stop in Denver for a few days, which was a welcome break for us. They were good to us but they being staunch Dutch Reformed felt so sorry for us, being hooked up with those Mormons, being misled, brainwashed. After many years we visit my Aunt Nellie [*Pieternella Weideman*] and Uncle Jacob [*Jacob Maten*] a number of time, but never got an opportunity to discuss the restored gospel of Jesus Christ.

One more day and night on the train through the beautiful route through the Rocky Mountains, arriving in Salt Lake 6 April 1930, just the day the church was 100 years organized. We settled down for a few days by Bro. and Sis Boogaard. This same evening I was taken to the tabernacle the first priesthood meeting I attended in this land of Zion. Although I could not understand what was said but I still can remember the spirit which prevailed there. I felt so good to be among my own people. Learning more about the history of the church and about all the persecutions the people has gone through and all the sacrifices they were willing to make and learn about the blessing and the growth of the church I thinking about the attitude of my Uncle and Aunt, although I believe they were sincere. Yet I feel that those who are professing to be first rate Christians are the enemies of the Church of Jesus Christ of Latter Days on many occasions.

Renting a home and buying second hand furniture was the first thing to do. Bro. and Sis. Boogaard left one year ahead of US. He speaking the language very well was a great help to us. We were baptized about the same time as they in den Helder, Holland and have been close friends since.

Getting my flying license for this country was the next thing. I was very lucky to have the assistance of Bro. Zappy who was running a furniture store and went with me to the airport to break me in this flying business. This was quite a problem. It took us four hours to answer 45 questions. I not knowing the language, he not knowing anything about airplanes. I tried to explain in Dutch, he translate in English. Anyway we made it and I was now able to fly in this country. Seventeen years later we were both on a mission in Holland.

The first ward we lived in, Forest Dale, Bishop Spencer, who has filled a mission in Holland as a young man, had helped us with wise counsel and warning pertaining to finances, he being the vice president of the Zion Savings Bank. In the meantime, doing some business in the bank there, we run into the first missionary who knock on our door in 1926 and introduced us to the gospel, and from that time on remained close friends. He had a job as a teller.

Moving out of that ward after eight months, I lost track of our first bishop. Then 26 years later, Ray Hutchenson, our first missionary, came to our home asking us if we were willing to take a job to take care of an old man who had lost his wife, and was looking for a middle age couple to live in his home and to take care of him, he being an invalid because of a stroke, he had a few years ago. Not knowing who he was, we went to that address and to our great surprise we found him to be our first bishop. He was really an invalid and needed help in everything day and night. We took care of him for the last seven months of his life. We lived in his home, we were well paid, but we were strictly tied up. He needed special cooked food and needed to be fed like a child. To keep him clean was a big job, especially during the night. Yet we could see he was gradually loosing ground and passed away at the age 87. This was the first time we attended the passing away of a person. Being reduced down and helpless as a child, death is then a blessing. We were offered to buy the home for a reasonable price. Being it a better home, we sold our own and after making many improvements, sold it again after living there for six years. Yet always for the experiences and the opportunity to serve we are grateful.

The Parleys 4th ward happened to be a very active ward. There I got my start in temple work and which has been my main activity for almost 20 years. First doing endowments and later on was called as an ordinance worker. This calling I have always taken seriously. How more I began to understand the meaning of temple work and all it comprises. I looked at it as something that would be far over my head.

As I was getting close to my retirement, and wonder what I was going to do, we had, after making many fine improvement on our home, of which we were very proud. Yet I could not have any kind of animals. We were looking some place with some ground to keep myself occupied with things I would like to do. One day we were riding around and as always seeking guidance. We passed by a little sign "House for Sale." Going another half mile, got a feeling to turn around and see where and what it was. Almost instantly the place appealed to me, just what I had in mind. Good size home, about one third acre, big chicken coop, six fruit trees, not way out in the country, but close to stores. Everything we were looking for. Yes, I could see a lot of work that needed to be done, but that is what I needed. I would not have liked it if everything would have been spic and span. It did not take us long to decide and made the deal. Sold our home on 21st south for a price which paid for all the work we had done, and bought this home on 7200 south 9th east. This we did about one half year before I retired. Many times I was asked what I was going to do after I stop working for Kennecott. My reply always was like this, "**I have been punching the time clock for many years. Now I am going to be free to go and to come as I** please." Never will I tie myself up, this was for sure. I would not live long enough to do all the things I want to do. So we both, with all the ambition, we went to work enjoying ourselves very much in the improvement we made. Raising all our fruit and garden stuff, the wife happy with her home. We bought a trailer home and began to travel and see the country. However, for some reason we never got the chickens or small animals we were planning to have.

After working very hard for about two years, I got a call to labor in the temple. I kept on going quite regular for proxy work, also gave some of my time to help finish the ward house. But this call three days a week was making me more tied down than I had promised to do two years ago. Gladly I accepted the call and began to wonder, how I would measure up to this quite demanding and sacred work. Coming in contact and feeling the influence of a dedicated group of men, so helpful and so rich background as you find in the house of the Lord. All my desire for my perpetual freedom was gone. It just proves again, you be willing to serve the Lord and acknowledge the hand of the Lord in all things, you will be blessed beyond measure.

Learning all one need to learn and to memorize, looked to me like a mountain. I felt like a pigmy compared with these old educated men. And although I was blessed with a good memory, yet I was very much self conscious, and standing before a group of people I was not used to, and the fear of getting stuck or of making mistakes did not help much, even I came to the point that it took away the appreciation for the privilege. I had to labor in the house of the Lord. Even I felt I could not go on. One day I kneeled down and told the Lord of my difficulty and asked to take away anxiety and have me relax. How grateful I am as, from that very moment I have never been bothered any more when making a mistake, of even on some days getting mixed up, I quietly tried to make correction without getting all riled up as before. How grateful I am for his help.

The association with the brethren has been so helpful in getting a better understanding of the endowment work. So many of these men having been bishops, stake presidents, some mission presidents, even a few who have filled 3 or 4 missions and have gained a great deal of scriptural knowledge. It is always uplifting to listen to their experiences and their testimonies. And I admit I felt myself often like a spiritual pigmy in comparison with them. Many of them in their private lives has occupied important positions in political field and as professionals, some are men of means, yet are willing to get up three o'clock in the morning give of their time and talents to serve in the house of the Lord.

I always will remember the statement made by one of the leaders, who has said during our regular prayer meeting, "Bretheren, remember this is a house of learning." Yes I thought, thinking about the things we need to memorize, but before long I learn the real meaning of his statement. This is the place to learn to be more humble, more willing to serve unselfishly, overcoming any degree of seeking glory for one self, and above all to forget one self. It has been stated that happiness come through unselfish service to the church and to our fellow men. I believe this to be true. Having had this privilege since 1965, I am grateful for the many wonderful experiences that has come to me.

Living as we were on 7200 south 9th east when I started to work in the temple. This travel to and fro, especially in the wintertime became for me more and more difficult and as we found it advisable to try to get closer to town, we began to look around and making, as usual, it a matter of prayer, we were in a distinct way led to an apartment close to the temple and very much agreeable to the wife. Here we were again moving for the eighth time since we came to this country. Fall 1966, we sold our home which we built up in such a nice place and where we were going to live for the rest of our lives, but again as many times before, there was a good reason to make the change. Apartment living was something we had to get used to, after for so many years having our own home. Yet getting older it has its benefits. Then after living 13 year in an apartment, we were counseled to put some of our saving in a place to call our own again.

Having a friend who was living in a mobile home park and pointing out the benefit to elderly couples of living in a mobile home park, made us decide to look around, and seek advice of some people we knew. We found a single 14 x 65 feet home, and are well satisfied. First, I have enough garden to keep me, during the season, occupied which I enjoy. Second, this part of the park is only for families without children and is very quiet. Third, we have a distinct feeling of safety, the park being fenced in. Bus connection right at the entrance of the gate, many stores and business places within walking distance. This place we bought Oct. 1978. Again we had to learn to adjust ourselves to this type of living which for me has not been a difficult matter. Because I had right away plans for improvements and as always has given me a measure of satisfaction. Although in order to fulfill my call in temple I had to travel about eight miles back and forth, but soon got used to it.

1983 - Approaching my 85 birthday I wonder sometimes how many more years I would be able to continue to labor in the house of the Lord. This has been such an important part of the last 18 years.

Looking back upon our 59 year of marriage life, with all the ups and downs, there is so much we should be thankful for, so much we should remember and talk about and try to push all our failings and mistakes in the background and keep on getting an understanding of each others needs.

Our Sons Jan [*John*] and Willem [*Bill*]

Eight October 1924 our first child was born. This happened sooner as I had wished for, not because I did not want to have children, but I was hoping for some time to get better to know my wife, and to adjust ourself to this whole new way of life. Our courtship had been so short, and I wanted so much to enjoy together those hobbies I did like so much. Riding my motorbike was one of them. Travel through the land on weekends. Having a pleasure boat was on my mind, reading good books together. I am afraid I was flying too high with my hobbies. All this in my mind was not going to be.

Not having close friends that time, no family in this town, and without the counsel of parents which we needed so bad and inexperienced as we were pertaining to pregnancy. I was groping in the dark, unprepared as we were, wrestling with problems I could not solve. This flying business I was in took so much of my thinking, nobody could understand, certainly not my young wife, who was going through that experience of pregnancy and asking for much attention, she was so much in need of, and must have felt many times of being neglected. The dangers of flying in those days was much on my mind, but we never talked about it. We very seldom had a free discussion of our secret thoughts, which did not help much.

When the time came our boy [*Jan Hendrik*] was to be born, (which at that time was common) in the home. Just the doctor, my mother and myself. It is not easy to express my thoughts, my feeling about witnessing the birth of a child. The suffering and pain which goes with bringing a child in the world. Almost a feeling of guilt of me being the cause of it, took away any kind of joy which I should have felt at that moment. Thinking why did we not wait until we would be more matured.

Of course, when it was all over and I looked at that clean and beautiful son of mine, I began to feel as a proud father. And realizing the wife apparently had come through this ordeal okay, and looked so happy, all those dark thoughts disappeared. Instead of thinking of my so called lost hobbies, all our attention went to the boy, who was growing up so fast. This was the time when we enjoyed the dog [Max, a large German Shepard], which was given as a present of her father. Very faithful dog and a protector of the wife and boy.

This boy just like his mother, I never knew what he would do next, and needed watching all the time from getting hurt. When he was three year old he got himself burned with hot water, the wife calling missionaries who administered to him and in a surprising short time he was healed.

By the time he was four years old and still no brother or sister to play with, we were longing for another child, hopefully a daughter. We were at that time fairly active in the branch and the principle of prayer was well established. As we went on our knees asking the Lord to bless us with another child. As we learn in due time the wife being pregnant, we felt so grateful the Lord has answered our prayers. That this happen to be a boy [*Willem Adriaan*] was no disappointment at all. Time enough to get us a daughter, but this was not to be the case. I have always felt this was something we have missed more than anything else.

This boy, Willem, was born in the navy hospital, 5 Sept. 1929 and we were grateful for the increase in the family. There was a difference of attitude. The first one too soon, the second one we have to pray for. Those boys being 5 year apart made the oldest the protector of the youngest. This however, made the youngest depend on the oldest more as was good for him. The oldest taking up the fight for the youngest, which kept him from fighting for himself.

I always was and still am deeply proud about my two sons. Perhaps not letting them know it as much as I should have. Not only proud but grateful as they have progressed, each in his own way, as they are in many ways two different personalities.

As they grow up on the farm, John from his nineth until his seventeenth when he went in the army, WW II. How we remember how he developed that inventive spirit and that spirit of adventure. We still can see him jumping with an old umbrella out of the hay barn on the hay wagon. Still remember how he fabricated a diving helmet and had me with an old bicycle pump, pump air to him when he was in 7-8 feet water. And even offered me to try it, which I wisely did not do. How he with a real seaman heart built a little boat he was very proud of, and so was I. And years later build one with which we made some wonderful trips, called the Green River Friendship Cruise, 117 miles down the Green River and 85 up stream the Colorado, never to be forgotten and will always to thankful for.

He had a desire to be a navy man (he must have it from his father), the disappointment not to be accepted. Then going in the army and have an eventful army career. I hope he will write about himself.

Looking back over those years when he was young, I regret not having more given of my time and interest. I am afraid I was asking too much work of him. It was with me as with my own father, too long hours, too little time for his boys. Yet the few times we broke away are always remembered. Our first trip to Yellowstone we will always remember. We got all the fish we could eat. We remember the nights we tried to sleep in our tent and how cold it was. How we were so fascinated to see those bears and even see them stand up to the car. This first time trip we remember the best. This mountain travel for those who came from the flat county like Holland is very inspiring and we have enjoyed the trip we made to Denver in our pickup truck. The boy old enough to drive, which made him feel important with his mother beside him, and Dad and his youngest son on an old car seat in the back, having the beauty sight, plus all the nice things to eat, and everybody was satisfied. How we learn to appreciate this great land. How I could be emotionally stirred on certain occasions when I heard the people sing the Star Spangled Banner. What a thrill this was.

Yes I do remember the times when that boy got on my nerves, and would to get hold of him and give him a licking, but he could run faster than I, and when I finally got hold of him, it was mother to smooth the things over again. One day I being very upset, he walk away and stayed away all night. Of course, none of us got any sleep, and when he came back next morning and told us he had slept in Tooele at the sheriff office, all was forgiven. And whenever he might be inclined to write his life story, I hope he will not be too tough on his father, hope he may come to realize the hard years, not only economically but emotionally and the great challenge facing his parents during those years on the farm. To try to be true and faithful, to the cause we came for. How easy we could have drifted away from the church, like so many who came from foreign land, and have taken whole families with them.

Yes I am sure I have demanded more as I should have. I demanded too much of myself and from Mom. Yet looking back I am grateful to the Lord for the obstacles we have overcome, and learned some hard lessons. He will never know how I have enjoyed and appreciated the wonderful trips with his boat on the river. How I have and always will be thankful for his willingness to do something for his mother. Always ready to help and do first things for us. As he is mechanically inclined and having an inventive nature, he would try anything that would be a challenge to him. And it has always been a pleasure to share with him, and to be of some help to him. I have rejoiced with him when a new promotion came along. The pride I felt to see him progress in his chosen occupation, his determination to reach the goals he has set. Perhaps I have been like my own father, who could brag about his sailor boy, especially after I became an aviator, but was very scarce of praise to the boy himself. Probably he figure I would get a swelling head if he would give me too much praise.

Will he ever know our anxiety when he went to war? Being exposed to all the influences of older and tougher men, the sever training he had to go through in the hot desert in Southern California and being in the tank division, being shipped out to England to take part in the invasion of Normandy. From here I will leave it to him to write his own story. I hope he will be inclined to do so. And may he know that the prayers of his parents in his behalf has gone with him wherever he has gone.

Much I have written about our oldest son goes also for our son Bill. We are proud of him in all his endeavors. He was the boy we prayed for. He has lived on the farm from the time he was four until he was sixteen, and has been under the influences of his 5 year older brother and in some ways did grow up in the shadow of him. How great it would have been for him if more brothers or sisters would have come but this was not to be so. He always will be remember of doing his part without being told. I believe he was sensitive to the struggle his parents went through. He as a healthy growing up boy, having his hobbies, and inclined to be a farmer or stock raiser if he would have a chance to go in that direction. We still see him leave for a three year stint in the coastguard and I did live over again the time I left home when I was 14. I was hoping at that time, he would make his career in that line. Yet there was something in that farm boy which kept him from gaining a love for the sea like his dad and brother. And I believe if he could have found his way and after coming out of the coastguard and could have settled on a farm, he would have found his life's work and would have been happy. As it has turned out, trying to find his life's work in all the kinds of occupations he has followed, never has given the satisfaction he should have had. Religious inclined more as his brother, has directed his life. Serving a mission to his native country has given him the challenging experience of missionary work and has been always active in the church. We hope he will write his life story for the benefit of his five children, of whom we are very proud.

Wish I had in their formative years given more attention, and did share more in their hopes and desires. But this is water under the bridge, a part of life.

Hendrik and Jacoba wedding day
December 12.1923
Rotterdam, South Holland, Netherlands

Jacoba, Jan (John), Hendrik Dinkelman
Den Helder, Holland circa 1928

Jacoba, Willem, Jan, Hendrik Dinkelman
shortly before leaving for America 1930

Jacoba and her boys
approx, 1934

John and the ever faithful dog Max. Max was given to the family by Jacoba's father. Max was devoted to John and when they would walk along the canals of Holland Max always maneuvered himself between John and the water to ensure John's safety. When John was horribly burned at the age of 2 Max stayed by his side watching over him. When the family came to America they had to leave poor Max behind.

Camping with her sons

The Family approx. early 1940's

Family Life   Members of

FATHER'S NAME DinkeLman.Hendrik BIRTH DATE 23-1-1898 DEATH DATE 22/11/

MOTHER'S NAME wachter. Jacoba BIRTH DATE 21-11-1903 DEATH DATE 14/01/

CHILDREN	BIRTH DATE	MATURE HEIGHT	MATURE WEIGHT	BODY BUILD*	HAIR COLOR	EYE COLOR	COMPI **
Jan. Hendrik	8-10-1924	6.2.	185	L	[DOD 09/10/2011]		
Willem Adriaan	5-9-1929	6.1.	180	L	[DOD 26/10/2002]		

MAM—DAD.

Jan Hendrik
1924

Willem Adriaan
1929

Religion   My Conversion

Everyone who has received a personal testimony of the fact that Jesus is the Christ, and that the Church of Jesus Christ of Latter-day Saints is his kingdom here on earth, has undergone a conversion process – it matters not whether he was "born under the covenant," in an L.D.S. home, or whether he was once a "stranger and a foreigner in the household of faith." Probably the most vital part of your history is the story of your conversion. After you fill in the suggested information on this subtopic sheet, you should be sure to write a detailed account of your conversion and testimony. An outline for that purpose is provided on the next page.

FILL IN THOSE BLANKS WHICH APPLY:

I (WAS, WAS NOT) BORN UNDER THE COVENANT *I was not born under the Covenant*

PLACE OF RESIDENCE WHEN CONVERTED *Den Helder N: Holl. Netherland*

MY FORMER CHURCH WAS *Dutch Herformed church* MY AGE *28*

DATE OF BAPTISM *1 Sept 1927* PLACE OF BAPTISM *North Sea.*

BY WHOM BAPTIZED *Reed Andrus Idaho* DATE OF CONFIRMATION *4 Sept 1927*

BY WHOM CONFIRMED *G. A. Grover, Idaho*

MY FIRST CONTACT WITH THE CHURCH *Spring 1926.*

DOCTRINES WHICH ATTRACTED ME *The babtisme for children*

STUDY & READING WHICH IMPRESSED ME *The Doctrine of Faith (The restoration* almass: 31-43 *of the gospell. Communication with the unseen which is proven to be possable. if we are in tones with the holy spirit impressed me the most*

DOUBTS, PROBLEMS, & HABITS I OVERCAME *The whole restauration of the gospell rest upon the vision in the grove. and all that has come forth the church as it is today has taking away any doubt I might have had. and without the book of mormon the church never would have grown as it has, because of those many who have been converted though that book. The problem of controlling the desires, appetite, and Passions according the boundries the Lord has set, has been the greatest*

MISSIONARIES OR OTHERS INVOLVED *challenge to me.*
Br Hutchinson and Br Rose has been the first missionaries who knocked on our door in 1926 – in Den Helder. Netherland Br Rose passed away. Br Ray Hutchinson and his "two best friends written Nov 15, 1977

CH. CALLINGS	DATE	BY WHOM SET APART	WARD AND STAKE

Baptized by Br. Reed Andrus, By George. A. Grover Confirmed

Gorden and Ray The first missionaries to knock on our Door
Albert the first missionary who took us down on our Knees

| Gorden Rose | Albert. Venema | Ray Hutchinson |

Hendrik, John and Jacoba late 1920's Holland
photo provided by Terry Wright, Boogaard's grandson

Jacoba fell in love with the motorcycle first
then Henk

approx, early 1950's

The Family in America Mid 1930's

circa. 1950's

circa.. 1980's

circa. late 1940's early 1950's

circa. 1980's

Hendrik and Jacoba 1983

circa. 1980's

List or Manifest of Alien Passengers for the United States of America
SS Nieuw Amsterdam
Sailing form Rotterdam   March 19, 1930

https://heritage.statueofliberty.org
also referenced in Family Search see
John Henry Dinkelman KWC7-2Y7 sources

First Name: Hendrik
Last Name: Dinkelman
Place of Birth: Holland
Date of Arrival: 1930
Age at Arrival: 32
Grnder: Male
Ship of Travel: Nieuw Amsterdam
Manifest Line Number: 22

First Name: Jacoba
Last Name: Dinkelman
Place of Birth: Holland
Date of Arrival: 1930
Age at Arrival: 26
Grnder: Female
Ship of Travel: Nieuw Amsterdam
Manifest Line Number: 23

First Name: Jan H
Last Name: Dinkelman
Place of Birth: Holland
Date of Arrival: 1930
Age at Arrival: 5
Grnder: Male
Ship of Travel: Nieuw Amsterdam
Manifest Line Number: 24

First Name: Willem A
Last Name: Dinkelman
Place of Birth: Holland
Date of Arrival: 1930
Age at Arrival: 5 months
Grnder: Male
Ship of Travel: Nieuw Amsterdam
Manifest Line Number: 25

SS Nieuw Amsterdam

Religion — Ordinances — Callings

ORDINANCE	DATE	BY WHOM PERFORMED	WARD AND STAKE
BLESSING			
BAPTISM	1 Sept 1927	Reed Andruss	Helder Branch – Holland
ORD. DEACON	20 Jan 1929	G. F. Hill	" " "
ORD. TEACHER	2 Feb 1930	John Sieverts	" " "
ORD. PRIEST			
ORD. ELDER	11 Jan. 1931	Agnes. B. Cannon	Forest Dale Ward. S L City
ORD. SEVENTY			
ORD. H. PRIEST	21 Feb. 1954	Franklin. L. Burton	Miller ward.
PAT. BLESSING	16 Dec 1930	Willard. Cushing Burton	Forest Dale Ward
ENDOWMENT	30 Jan. 1934	Joseph Christenson	Pres: Salt Lake Temple
MARRIAGE	12 Dec. 1923	Civil Marriage	Rotterdam. Holland
SEALING	30 Jan 1934	Joseph Christenson	Pres: Salt Lake Temple
Pat Blessing	11 March 1947	Franklin. B. Woodbury	Milcreek. ward.

CH. CALLINGS	DATE	BY WHOM SET APART	WARD AND STAKE
Home teaching		Bishop Spencer	Forest Dale Ward
Home teaching		Bishop Bangerter	Granger Ward
Elder Quorum		Bishop John Hill.	" "
Elder Quorum		Bishop Little	milcreek Ward
mission Call	23 march 1947	" "	" "
Sunday shool Pres.		Bishop R. Brems	miller Ward
Secretaris H. Priest	21 Feb. 1954	" " "	" "
ward clerck	" "	" " "	" "
Home teaching, Genealogical Committy		Bishop Beuner	Parleys Forth Ward Parley stake
Ordinance worker	16 aug 1965	Pres. McDonald	S. L Temple, from Union 2nd Ward
Ward Clerck	Feb 1967 – Feb 1975	Bishop Hunter	17th ward. S. Lake stake
H. P. Secretaris	Feb 1975 – nov 1979	Bishop Mills	" " "

Family Life   Our Homes

It is suggested that a photo, drawing, or description of each house you have lived in be shown on this page. For each one give its complete address. Depending on available space, you may want to show photos or sketches of backyard views, inside views, special rooms, floor plans, etc.

No. 28 Is the home of my Birth 23 of January 1898 Two room and a atick devided in two. 5 Boys and 5 girls where born in this Home

on No. 26 lived a jewish Fam: as a boy I had the job on the jewish sabbath to light the fire and to keep the fire going during the day. in the evening to lighten the oil lamp and the candle. made 15 cents

Bakkerstraat No. 28
Hilversum
Holland

Our home in Den Helder Jan in t Veltstraat 53. In this home the gospel was introduced by Brother Ray Hutchinson and Brother Rose. Missionarys of the church of Jesus Christ. during the summer of 1926

This home 1920 South 4th East Salt Lake City we bought for $1250. everthing included Furniture, chicken Coope with 80 chickens. We lived here from Dec 1930 untill april 1933. After making many improve. ments We traded this home in as first pay on the 27 acres farm in Granger for $2750. Wich left us in debt of $3000.

[1930-1933]

This is our home on the farm in Granger We lived here from april 1933 untell 1944 We bought this for 5000 dollar and sold it for 7000. Just a smal profit for all the improvement I have made during those Eleve year. This lantoo plus hot and cold water and water toilett was build bij me and the boys to the great satifation of mother and all of us, many rich experiences we have had. Good and bad, for both we are still greatfull. 4090 West 3500 South Grang

[1933-1944]

This has been our home from 1944 untill 1950. This Place about 1 1/2 acre was just we were looking for. It had a nice Barn to keep smal animals, some nice fruit trees plenty of Irrigation water to grow all the vegetables we needed. This place will always be remembered for all the tree cutting the boys and I have done. eleven of these big poplar trees (like this one) we cut down and burned them up. and planted young ones. from this home we were called on our mission. Bought for 5900. solt in 1950 for 15000 3775 South seven East

This home we both for 9300 dollar, very close to the bus line. between Main and State street. Just big enough for two of us as the boys got already married. This home I made improvements. build a garag 40 feet by 16 feet wich did gave me a nice work shop. here we were going to live the rest of our life. But the Lord just had it planned different. as we were called to render service to the man who happen to be our first Bishop when we came to this country Solt this home for 13000 in 1956

[1950-1956]   36 Miller ave. 3175 S° Main

This is our last home we owned, Bought in March 1962 for 18000 Solt Nov 1966 for 21000
Much work we have done on this home. Wich has given me much satisfaction. This home had five (5) rooms, Pluss a nice room to be used as a office. This place about 3/4 of a acre had six fruit trees, big garden; big chicken coope. a perfect set up for a man, who was going to be retired.
[1962-1966]   addres 7150 S° 9th East Union

This home we bought 13500 in aug 1956 and solt for 16750 Nov 1962
addres 2002 East 21st South S.L City
It was in this home we took care of the man who happen to be our first Bischop, the last seven month of his life. This home had a full unfinesh Basement, wich we finished in a very nice way, and we were proud of our work. 21st south is a very busy road, we have on certain times of the day Clocked 105 cars in 5 min:
[1956-1962]

Kensington Apartments 180 North Main SLC

After selling the home in Midvale, Utah they moved to the Kensignton Apartments in downtown Salt Lake City, then to a trailer community in North Salt Lake, then back to downtown Salt Lake to be near the temple, then to Millcreek in the Colonial Apartments where they remained until Hendirk passed away. Jacoba eventually moved to a close by senior community where she remained until her passing.

2nd North between West Temple and Second West SLC

Colonial Apartments 4759 S 1300 E Millcreek

Brightly Beams our Fathers

Brightly Beams our Father's mercy
 From his lighthouse ever more,
But to us he gaves the Keeping
 Of the Lights along the shore.

Dark the night of sin has settled;
 Loud the angry billows roar.
Eager eyes are wathing Longing,
 For the lights along the shore.

Trim your Feeble lamp my Brother,
 Some poor Sailor Tempest Lost,
Trying now to make the harbor
 In the darknes may be lost.

  Led the lower lights be burning
  Send a gleam across the wave
  Some poor struggling seaman.
  You may rescue you may Save

This song was the first song I heard singing, and at that time
made a diep impression (unknown) me. As at that time of my life
I was as it were that struggling seaman, looking
for something to hold onto Spiritualy speaking. This I
found in that (at that time) disrespectfull mormon church

Our Life on the Farm

1933-1944

During the winter 1932-33, the flying business was going down more and more and I could see the handwriting on the wall. Although picking up in the spring, but not enough to have work for three pilots. I became discouraged because we were already three months behind in wages. Money to keep the planes in proper repair was hard to get. It all worked to make me look for a change in my life. Getting a pilot job on one of the regular airlines was out of the question as so many pilots were out of work, and I was getting too old to be considered.

Now it would be kind of strange to tell that when I was a young boy and was asked what I was going to be, the answer was always, "I am going to be a farmer." Perhaps because I could be so busy helping Dad with his garden and his hogs, planted in me a desire to be a farmer. Now don't ask me why I have to be a navy man for 18 years before my desire to become a farmer became a reality. Yet circumstances did lead me in that direction.

Let me go back a few years. We arrived April, 1930 in Salt Lake. We rent a home for about 6 month. We had a chance to buy a little home from an old railroadman who could not take care for himself anymore. This home was rundown and very dirty. But we knew how to fix and to clean it. We were happy to have our own home. This home we bought for $1000 and $250 for all the furniture, tools and chickens. After two years, making many improvements, we turn this home as a down payment on a 27 acre farm. It paid me well for all the work I had done. In the spring 1933, making the decision to buy a farm, we could sell this home (after having made a lot of improvement) for a profit as a down payment to the elderly couple who owned the farm. They were happy and we were too. That this home had negro neighbors on both sides, this did not matter to us, as we had no prejudice against black people. They were good people. But to sell a home like that kept many Americans from buying.

May 1933, we made the deal and moved to the farm. I was still keeping my job as a flyer, until August 1933. I had made acquaintance with a 17 year old farmers boy, who was trying to work himself in aviation. He was willing to live with us and help me break myself in this farming business. I know it sounds unbelievable, but here stood a man knowing absolute nothing about farming, not the least about how to handle horses, and we had three, did not know how to put a harness on, knew nothing about what or how to cultivate a crop. (Luckily this was already planted by the owner.)

I am grateful to this young boy who broke me in during the first 4 months, and who is, after almost 50 years, one of our best friends.

We were starting an altogether different life and with all my ambition and enthusiasm learning every day a little more and willing to work long hours. I gradually got the hang of it. We had some very helpful neighbors who were giving good advice and sometimes the help we needed.

Now this farm located in Granger, about 10 mile west of Salt Lake City, was at that time sparsely populated. There was only one ward in whole Granger area. The place was much run down. The land has been neglected, much was to be done on the farm and buildings. The house was a very modest home without any conveniences, such as cold and warm water, no toilet, no bathroom of any kind. We felt like pioneers just starting a homestead. Yet we did not become discouraged, full of ideals, we were making this farm the best place to live. I was now my own boss and was going to live here for the rest of my life.

Luckily I was more or less blind of the negative conditions, that I and the wife and boys would have to work long and hard did not matter. I was now a free man and having faith to be guided and directed kept us overcoming setbacks and disappointments, which were many. Unprepared as I was, I made many mistakes and poor judgement, at times overworking myself, which made things worse. Yet the ideal to make this farm a high producing place did not leave me, regardless the severe setbacks. For example, I spent almost our last dollar buying lumber for a large chicken coop, of which we were very proud, and making the mistake of not tying it down in the ground with steel wire, a severe duststorm blew the whole coop to pieces. This duststorm did a great deal of damage all around the country. A few days later the elders of the ward came together and helped me to put the coop together again. This sure strengthen my faith in the priesthood. Loosing one of our nice producing cows just ready to give a calf, died. The wife had to go to the hospital for an operation, denied us to have more children, especially a daughter. One more cow did blow and died.

Now it is not difficult to imagine what kind of ideas the people had of that Dutch fellow who knew nothing about farming, and was trying to make a living on a poor rundown 27 acre farm in the poorest time of the history. And if it was not for the little savings we had, we could have never made it. Yet it left us with $3000 mortgage with 4 percent interest. We only had to pay $20 a month on the principle and interest. But I could not even make that. In Aug. 1933, I quit flying. That young man who was with us got a job and left us. By the way he became later on a very experience pilot.

Together with the wife and our 11 year old boy we had quite a struggle ahead of us. We had always plenty to eat, but cash money was so hard to get. Whatever we raised brought in such a little

bit of money. The full milk gave us 11cents the gallon, one bushel of finest wheat was only 45 cent with, first grade porkers brought only four and one half cent on foot, nice six week weaner pigs sold for one dollar, if you could find a buyer, one dozen eggs 18-19 cent. The water situation was very poor, and grasshoppers were taking their share from what little hay I raised. On top of all our trouble we lost one of our horses who got himself upside down in a ditch and died.

It seemed like the Lord was testing this man to the limit. This man who left with his wife and two boys, his native country, leaving a high paid job, so called for the sake of the gospel, and who at that period of his life was not as faithful in living the law of tithing. Even if it was not much we were making.

I planted 5 acres in sugar beets. We got $28 credit from the sugar factory for seed and fertilizer. And by the way of the white fly, this was a total failure. And I was still in debt for the seed and fertilizer. Many men were on relief, we never had to do, I was too proud. But the chance to loose the farm was my greatest concern.

It was at that time (1934) President Roosevelt instituted the federal land bank, giving loans to those who were in need to save their farms. Getting this loan helped me so much, because we did not pay on the principle, only 4 percent interest every three month for the next three years. It also seem the Lord was putting us to the test if we were longing to be back to our native country. Or we would lose faith in the words of Apostle Widstoe who had said "Brother go," after his counsel was asked for.

I never had the desire to be back. I found so much freedom here. Perhaps I was too proud to admit defeat. I also know by leaving the service I had burned the bridges behind me. Or did I really have that much faith in the land of Zion? I did not know, probably a mixture of all three. 1934-1935 was the lowest time of our existence on the farm, from then on things were slowly getting better for us.

While I was in debt to my neighbor for $22 for three load of hay it was hard to scrape that money together and as he needed the money to pay the water assessment. I pray the Lord to open the way for me to earn that money. Our friend Brother Boogaard, who was a carpenter, came to see me. He needed some help to put a concrete foundation under a home. He figure 2-3 days. Glady I accept his call for four dollars a day. Starting Monday up to Friday, then have to come back Saturday for a half day. This was five and a half day, exactly $22. I then became aware that my prayer was answered just as I had asked for, and felt thankful to the Lord, as I again knew that sincere prayer never fails.

[The following insert was provided by Terry Wright, who is the grandson of Marinus and Minna Boogaard. It provides additional information to this story. The Boogaards were baptized at the same time as Dinkelmans and remained life long friends.]

On 8 February 1984, as we met at Henry's home following Marinus' funeral, the Boogaard family's very good friend, Henry Dinkleman, pages 136-137, related the following incident that describes conditions during the Depression in a poignant way. "Were very poor, 33 and 34 were the lowest years I can think of. Hardly any water, 'n the grasshoppers were sooo bad. So I didn't have enough hay for my cows. Went to my neighbor across the street, he has only one cow, 'n he had some hay to sell. I said, Tom, I says, I need some hay. He said you go in the field load up, 'n take it to the scale. 'N I took about three loads of hay from him. That took twenty-two dollars, three load of hay. Well, a, he said you don't need to pay me now. He said, I would like to have the money when the Water Assessment comes due, in November or October. I said, oh no, that was June uno, so I should make that. Went along, in August still no twenty-two dollars. September no twenty-two dollars. 'N that debt was so on my mind, to get that twenty-two dollars to pay on that hay. 'N then came October, a, I was worrying about it. We went down on our knees 'n asked the Lord to open the way that I could make that twenty-two dollars to pay the debt off. Very simple uno, just right off the bat he (Marinus) comes down to my place. He said Hank, he says, I need some help. I got to, 'n concrete 'n cement, a, underneath 'n house that was standing on, under some blocks. He said I need some help, make forms, 'n pour the concrete, all by hand. He said Oh, maybe two days. Thought we could do it in two days. 'N I forgot all about the question of me asking the Lord to help, make me earn the twenty two dollars. I said, Yah sure, there I went, boy I work like heck. Crawling on my knees, that how I get those rocks away, get the forms in. Well, three days at least at four dollars a day. Four dollars a day. 'N then he said, well I need you tomorrow too. O. K., I'll be there. 'N then Friday, that makes Monday, Tuesday, Wednesday, Thursday 'n Friday. That's five days, twenty dollars. Friday night he said I got to have you tomorrow too. I got Saturday morning back, work four hours for two dollars. 'N that's just exactly twenty-two dollars. 'N, Earl, right then I became conscious of the fact that we have asked the Lord to open the way to earn twenty-two dollars." I then asked Mr. Dinkleman if he, Marinus, had known about he and Koos praying for help. He said, "no, no, I told him later on he saved my life. He have been an instrument in the hand of the Lord to help with the way to make me that twenty-two dollars."

Andy was sitting next to us during the tape recording and made the following comment. "A little back up on that. Grandpa (Andy's father) was moving a house for the Postmaster, Glassett, 'n he couldn't pay the rent (on the Glassett home they were then living in). He was having trouble, so he was working to pay his rent to keep on this task of putting a new foundation under the whole thing, so he got rent plus a few dollars. That was on Seventh East about 30th South." Andy and Hank's son, John, were very good friends and played together for many years as young boys. Some very humorous boyhood escapades occurred with these two.

After struggling through the first six years, the wife had unknown to me, saved $400 and bought a tractor. What progress that was for me. Sold the horses and glad to get rid of them because one was lazy and the other was crazy, never knew when to stop.

I am still in debt to my son who did milk the cows better than I ever did learn. Even the wife was going to learn to milk. But after one unruly cow got his leg in the bucket and she in the cutter, that was the end of her milking. Yet she did so much to help me through those difficult days. Making work horse of myself, not enough rest made me not easy to get along with. Spending so much time trying to get some water on the land and spending so little time with my sons.

It was for all of us a relief when in 1936 the copper industry started up. I with the help of a neighbor got a job, and although it was the lowest paid job yet I was thankful to the Lord.

All that hard work with that worn out equipment, the worst thing I did was demanding too much from my son Jan. Although after we got that tractor, he loved to run it and did a lot of work.

As we had more money coming in, everything went our way, better crops, better prices, more luck with animals, especially with raising hogs. Our youngest son, Bill, started to do little jobs which was a big help to his mother.

About my 25 years for Kennecott I will write a special chapter.

1936. Started to work for Kennecott, which came just in time, as we from now on had to pay on the principle, which was now no problem. Getting a better paid job, the farm producing better crops. We were appreciating the progress we were making. Even we could afford a trip to Yellowstone Park, which was for us something out of this world.

The joy we felt having the barn filled to the top with 40 ton of hay. The joy seeing the old sow giving us a litter of little ones, and see them coming in the world, and the boys saying "another one, were another one." Even some we have to take in the house and feed them with a bottle. How we would walk through the field and see the full stand of grain coming up, with the promise of a good crop. What joy as a heffer calf was born and most time it became a pet to the kids.

Having more money to spend, we started on a building project. We tore the old adobe kitchen down and started a nice lean-to on the house, getting water, toilet and shower, hot and cold water. Got a better car to travel, not being dependent on the farm income. We had so much to be thankful for. So many things happen some of these we still can talk about with pleasure.

We will never forget the day that I was going to butcher the first hog. The hog killer who comes around with his hot water and the proper tools did charge one dollar. Of course, as thrifty as I was, I was going to earn that dollar myself. All the preparation was made. A 50 gallon barrel stood on the fire, rope and rope block was ready, knife was sharp. All we needed now was more courage. I felt like a murderer, to kill my own raised hog. Well no use to cry. We just had made up our mind that you could not keep on feeding that hog forever, and if I sold that poor animal it would be killed anyway.

John gave me that hammer and be ready to hand me the knife. With the head of the hog between the knees, hit the head, and of course on the wrong spot of the head, and instead of stunting it, there she went squealing all over the neighborhood. After chasing her and again getting her between the knees, I was not going to make the same mistake again. Giving a big hit with the hammer, I just kept on hitting, and that was a bloody mess. And as the killing was such a poor job, the cleaning job was not any better, because the water was not hot enough. We just had to shave that darn hog, but some hair on the bacon did not matter much. Killing a bull was much easier. Those dumb animals are just standing waiting to be hit.

As a good farmer I wanted to learn all that a farmer should be able to do, such as smoking your own pork. I built a smoke house, got apple wood, built a fire and hung up the hams and bacon. Of course something had to go wrong. The fire, instead makes smoke was giving flames. Before I know it the strings burned through and everything was laying in the fire. Building all over again, we had the best hams and bacon ever smoked. We learned everything the hard way.

We lived on the farm from May 1933 until the summer of 1944, sold the place with a small profit. But all the 'experience we got was the biggest reward. And after many years looking back we are inclined to look upon all the trials and frustration we went through, all the setback, all the pressure during the years of the great depression, as being part of the school of life.

Some rather forgotten. Such as the time I was overworking myself to the limit and things not going as I wanted to. I could be a very bad example to the wife and to the boys. I could so easy lose control of my tongue and could use the name of the

Lord in vain so bad. When for instance a cow got through a fence, something of the equipment broke, or any other thing that would upset me. Then again coming to my senses I could feel so guilty, so unworthy. I could wish the end would come.

One Sunday I went to meeting alone, very much despondent, very much feeling my unworthiness. The man who was called to speak, spoke only about the great sin of taking name of the Lord in vain. I felt he was only speaking to me. All I wanted to do is to walk away. And going home walking in the dark street I lifted my hand in the air, and in all the despair of my soul I prayed. "Please Lord let me never use thy name in vain anymore." A calm feeling came over me, and from that very day, whenever I became upset or would start loosing my temper, there is an influence, power which kept me from using His name in vain. How grateful I am for this faith promoting experience, how it has strengthened my faith in prayer.

Being a Dutchman, well known for their bull headiness, always trying to accomplish things by his own power, had to learn the hard way that only in the last instance calling upon the Lord for help brings much grief. I need to learn to seek the help of the Lord always in sincere prayer and learn to be more humble, this being the way to successful living. So it is in every assignment we receive in the church, as well with every challenge we have to meet in our daily life.

I like to think back to the pleasant experiences, the simple things, such as going out to the lake and get all the carp we could carry. The wife being able to put them in bottles and make them so tasty to eat. The root beer she could make. Sometimes too strong so a bottle would explode, which gave a big scare. I remember John riding a horse in the corral and the horse running in the barn and John thrown off in the manure, and I don't remember if mom let him come in the house.

I remember the bull getting out on the road and pounding his feet at the door of some neighbors home, and going after him with a club and getting him home. We remember when we thought one of our horses was gone and after chasing all over the county found the horse in the barn.

I remember we not even having a lock on the door, never the least concern about stealing. What difference as I am writing this in 1982. That wonderful feeling of freedom when we could drive a car without a license. Taxes was our least worry.

I remember the time we for the first time went during a political gathering to Salt Air and see that famous dance floor. We received a ticket at the entrance for a lottery that would be held and I received ten silver dollars. I almost fainted. One dollar for tithing, one dollar to pay the one we borrowed to get gas for the car. Life was so simple.

It was a special occasion when we went to see Gone with the Wind. All our recreation was found the first year in the ward and they could be wonderful evenings.

I remember when we went fishing in a canal and got some stuff when the boys were small. I could go on and on recalling all the simple pleasures.

I remember John when he built himself a diving helmet attached to a garden hose and foot pump. Going to a spot where 7-8 feet water was found and I standing there pumping my heart out to keep enough air to him and have to stop to get him come up again. The invitation to try it myself was politely not accepted. That boy of ours was as a teenager quite a guy. Full of life, always inventing, always tinkering with something, building ships was and is one of his hobbies. His heart was on the ocean, just like his father when he was young. We still treasure a picture of him in his seascout uniform. Later in years I have regretted so much for not having been closer to my two sons. There was so much in them I could have enjoyed together.

Our youngest son, who was only 4 years when we made the move, and he spent his growing years on the farm. I believe if things had been just right he would have gone in farming or ranching and stock raising. I believe he had the inclination. His hobby as young as he was, was raising rabbits and made him some nice rabbit pens. We remember those boys making some kind of parachute and jumping out of the hay barn on a load of hay.

We also killed five hogs in one day and what a satisfaction after a hard day work, to have 10 halves, nice looking hogs hanging in a row and buyers coming to buy a hog.

Another event took place which caused a lot of laughter. I wrote about one of our horses got up side down in a deep ditch. After a lot of help we got him out and brought the horse in the corral, and cover it up with straw, hoping he would come out of it. We had to go away for something and coming back we found one dollar bill inside the door. Then we saw our dog with some blood on his face. Something was not right. Going to the corral we found a lot of blood and the horse missing. This was a mystery to us.

Now it happened one half block away, that the farmer had a dead horse. He called the fish hatchery to haul away that dead animal. They came out and got mixed up and happened to come to our place, seen that sick horse and figure that was the one they were looking for. Cut the throat to bleed. Put a dollar in the house and went away. The farmer called again, when are you going to get my horse." "We already got it." "No sir, it is still here." Mystery solved.

I hope I have given some idea of our life on the farm, and as of all things this must come to the end. The second world war 1941 took our son Jan in the army and left home. My job at the copper industry gave much overtime. The wife working in the ammunition plant, and many other things made us feel the time has come to sell out and find a small place, which we did in 1944. And my dream farm came to an end. Yet with all the ups and downs we are grateful for all the experiences we have had, and all the hard lessons we have learned.

This History Is Mine

This Looked good

Our Pride

Our first grain crop

Hard work

Harold my right hand

We were all Proud of his work, Bill

argement Between Father-Son

This was for us such an excited day
to see all that grain coming out the thresher
But the price being so low was disheartening

our best jersey cows

BLOWING straw in the barn

Harold Spencer spreading the manour

our farm yard after we built the leantoe
on the house, out side gramy still there
on top & Boys schoolhus in the highway
our ford 1929 4 door, behind the sheds
our garden ground

This is our hay and grain grand

our milk coats. on 3700 so 4th east

on top of the Timpanogos 1938

on the old mare

H. 1933

Sending clothing and footstuff to
the folks soon after the war 1945

Hay raidy to heal in

My 25 Years Service by Kennecott Copper Co.

October 1936 - March 1963

I was very much in need of a job to get some cash income after struggling on the farm for three years. With the help of a neighbor who was well acquainted with the fellow who had the authority to hire workers of all kinds of trades that was needed when the copper plant started up after five years of reduced operation. I knew no trade but flying, and that was least they needed.

Starting on the bottom, I got a job on the 12 mile tailing pond. This dyke needed to be raised to hold the tailings. This was done by railroad car loaded with mine waste. Raising the track was done by manual labor, so also the unloading of the car, which was hard work. This was, of course, common labor and paid the lowest wages 45 cents an hour.

This was outside work and not having any protection from the weather. We were exposed even to eat our lunch, at times, in wind and rain, and seven days a week, and as you desire to stay home Sunday, you got the answer like this "you stay home Sunday, but don't come back Monday morning." Working conditions were very poor.

It was late in the fall and running in a nasty snowstorm, we were soaked and hungry, waiting for the motor car to pick us up. This motor car had great difficulty to get through the snow, it was getting late but we were just paid straight time.

Overtime, sick leave, pension, seniority plan, hospital care for the family, paid holidays, were not in existence at all. Job security we did not know of. Yet, after all we left in our native country, I thank the Lord for I have finally been able to get on the payroll. It is very difficult to make the youth of today understand the working conditions of those years. If they could get a clear picture, they would have a deep appreciation for all the sacrifices suffered by those who have brought to pass all the improved working conditions, especially in safety rules.

This company began in 1905 and in a primitive way, with the tools and equipment of the day, mostly finding the labor force among the imported Japanese, Chinese and Greek people.

After nine weeks, I got a job on the car dump, during the winter of 1936-37. Unloading those 100 ton loaded ore cars were pushed two at a time on a turn table and turned upside down. In winter when the ore froze, it was up to us to knock with long bars this ore out. At times nothing would come out as it was frozen so tight. Then with big gas torches we needed to heat the sides. All of this was work which paid better wages, but it was shiftwork, but having a warm place to eat our lunches, and were paid one and a half from time overtime.

Spring 1937. It was my luck to get a job as pipefitter helper in the pipe shop. I felt thankful, again better pay, straight days and the opportunity to learn a trade. In the mill, one finds miles of all kinds of pipes, big and small. Most were up in the ceiling or under floors and much of pipework was hard and dirty work, especially under the concrete floors.

But as jobs were to be done all over the plant we were not long in the same place. It was my fortune to be the helper to a very able pipefitter, Jack Marlor, who had a liking to this hard working Dutchman and who was willing to learn. This man taught me the tricks of the trade. It was also my fortune to work with him on all the company houses and got quite often in plumbing work, which did help me in later years.

Making another step upward, I became the threading machine man, also taking care of the shop. This job took me away from much hard and dirty work and again better pay. The principle of apprenticeship did not exist. Only when needed and boss figure you could do the work, you might have a chance to be put up as journeyman and make the full wages. I was at that time passed forty years old.

The company started to build a power house which would open up a number of new jobs. This started in 1941, when the war was on. I had some idea, as time went on, that there might be a chance to get a better job when the plant would go in operation. At the time they were looking for men to operate the plant, they had need of a labor foremen, to run a gang of laborers, and handle the coal business. I got that job and even took a little cut in pay, but I would be away from that heavy work.

I started four months before they started up, but as time went on they change the policies and they gave the choice to work in the maintenance department. This was the thing for me, because with the experience I got, did very well in that maintenance work and before long I was set up as a pipefitter journeyman, which job I kept till I retired 19 years later.

Many of the bosses were men from the east coast and had experience in running a power plant. As we all were new in this work, it took sometime to get organized and to learn that there were plenty of chance to get hurt. Working around high pressure steam, electricity and acid is not without risk. One time it being my job to hook up for unloading a tank car of sulfuric acid, which is done under pressure, a mishap happen and I got badly burned with that wicked stuff. Luckily water was close by and was a big help to counteract the burning.

Whenever something sprung a leak or broke, it was with all hurry to repair, and stay on the job to get it done, and many times we did run in overtime, sometimes in extra shifts. The plant had one 75000, one 50000, two 25000 KW generators. Each year one or two needed to be overhauled.

This was the busiest time of the year, working seven days, 10 hours a day, for about six weeks. This gave us good size pay checks, but it was also very tiresome. Even we got us a brand new car, feeling so grateful for the progress we have made. Sometime the wife and I could say to each other (thinking back the years of our trials and hardships), "Remember when we were hoping for the time to get a whole new set of tires on the car or that ever the time would come to have a whole new car" And now the time had come, and we were thankful to the Lord.

Yet I have always looked upon the trying years as a period of being tested or we would remain true and faithful to the cause we had come to this country, even though we were not without our weaknesses. Yet we did learn to see the hand of the Lord in all our experiences. And unknowingly, we were preparing ourselves for a call to fill a mission. Prosperous as we were, the farm was paid for, a good paying job, the wife worked during the war in an ammunition plant for about 13 month. Our oldest son in the army. Now the time has come to be tested or we would be willing to sacrifice for the sake of the gospel. The gospel that has guided and directed us since we accepted it.

All my life and in all my activities, I feel I have been directed, at times going in a different direction than I really wanted to go. After living on the farm for 11 years, time has come to make, again, a change. Both boys in the service, me a full time job. It was too much for us, although most animals were gone. Raising a crop became easier, much of the ground was rented out, yet we made the decision to sell out and to get a small place where I still could satisfy my desire to have small animals.

When the mission call came, I was 49 years old and had worked for the company 10 and a half years.

Telling superintendent I had accepted a mission for the church, he wish me good luck, which surprised me as he was a high up mason. Among my fellow workers, some LDS wished me success. Yet some of the guys thought I was not too well in the head. Explaining to me that when I would get back I would be passed fifty and chances to get rehired was out of the picture and what was I going to do after my savings were spent on a mission. They had some good arguments and were well meaning, except they don't know the ways of the Lord.

Coming back from our mission, I wrote a short letter to let the big boss know I was back and looking for a job. "Come and see me," and after a short conversation, he sent me to the doctor to pass a physical test which was the rule and next morning I was back on the job, the same job I had when I left. It was like I have never been away. Three different fellows had worked that job. The third one was ready to get another job and was glad I was back. Everything fell in place, as to always will if we are willing to serve the Lord.

After working 13 more years and coming to retirement age, I became concerned about the ten and a half years I served before I left on my mission. During those years a pension plan came into being and I wanted those years added to the 13 years I served after I came back. No matter who I saw, no matter what way I went, the answer was always "NO", as it was against the policy of the company.

During the war many fellows left the company to get higher paid jobs. Then after the war they came back but had lost their seniority and started again from the bottom. I was quite anxious to get those years added and we made it a question of prayer. It just happened one of the many strikes was going on and most unions did settle. The small electrical union of the powerhouse being the last one.

Denny Collings was negotiator for our union and was holding out for me, but they would be willing to give me those years, but had no power to do so. So, it finally went to the highest man in New York. After explaining that I did not leave the company to seek a higher paid job, but had left to serve his church, spending his own money on a mission and felt I should have those years for my pension. A telegram came back with a message "Give that man those years and let us go back to work".

This man, Denny Collings, and I met every so often in the temple and we always would bring up that faith promoting event and express my thankfulness for his persistence in getting for me that pension, which I enjoy at this time of writing (1982) for 19 years.

We had the hand of the Lord in this and again felt the true of this statement "You serve the Lord the best you know how and the Lord will take care of you".

On one occasion again being on strike, which was almost every 3 years, two jobs as watchman were opened for the two oldest in seniority. Both declined because it would be only for a few weeks. I was next in line and accepted, even took a cut in wages. Yet I think the Lord know what was for me, as the strike went on for five and a half months. This was a very easy job, only making the rounds every so often and keeping the fire equipment in shape and fire line flushing. This was a night shift and gave me plenty of time to keep up the farm.

A few years later, again being on strike, after we left the farm, I was wondering what I was going to do. Very shortly, Bishop Clarence Buehner offered me a job to help a carpenter who took a contract to build on the ward a bishop's office just what I love to do. I worked for six weeks and made 600 dollars. Now what was I going to do because the strike was still going on.

Brother Anderson asked me to do a job for him. He had an unfinished basement room and wanted me to finish a play and TV room. I had much pleasure in this job as I could work my own idea, paneling the wall, tile on the ceiling, and on the floor, build a nice fireplace and I was proud of the job and after taking four weeks and making $400 the strike was over and did not lose a day work.

We both felt so greatly blessed and again felt the hand of the Lord, and it strengthen our testimony, that if we will live the law of tithing, one never need to be afraid of going without the things we are in need of. I do not mean to say that one should live the law of tithing for material reason. But I am sure we will reap the blessings of being obedient to this law, as well any other law which we are taught to obey.

In those years I have worked for this company, I have seen many great changes in working condition. Safety rules was a great improvement. Although it must be gained through strikes, which for many was hardship and sacrifice and as we are the recipient of the sacrifices of our forefather pioneers, many of those now working for the company are benefited by the results of those strikes. Not that I was strike happy, but I know without them we never would have the blessings of our work as we have now.

I feel thankful for the years I have worked for this company. I retired the first of March 1963 and am wearing with pleasure, the gold watch given to me by the men I worked with all those years.

That day the fellows of the shop came together for a few minutes to wish me good luck and after receiving that watch, I experienced for the second time in my life of being tongue tied and felt embarrassed, but could not say a word. My pension for those 24 years work was only $54 a month, not too much. But every time a pay raise come along, so my pension got an increase, which is now $203 and am thankful to have that much come in each month.

Time to punch out

going Home

March 1963

This old Dutch Pipefitter
maindenance men

25000 KW Generator

on the Bridge

High Presser Waterpump

Our Mission to the Netherlands for the Church of Jesus Christ of Latter-Day Saints

March 1947-1949

I was called by Bishop Little of the Millcreek Ward, Cottonwood Stake being then 49 years old.

After accepting the call, I will never forget the struggle I had the first night with adversary, who is as real as anything can be real, whose power is great. All night long he let me feel that I was not worthy, that I was not capable, that I did not know enough to present the gospel to the people. As I really did not feel of myself being well equipped with knowledge of the scripture, I became very much disturb. I never in my life have experienced such a darkness and kept on asking the Lord if I am not worthy, that something will happen to keep me from going. This dark spirit which is so real and so overpowering was with me until by day light it left me and all became light within my soul.

Since that experience I began to understand at least partly what the boy Joseph Smith has gone through, before he kneeled down in the grove, how Satan did all he could to keep him from praying, realizing what would come forth from his first prayer. Yet how terrible it was, I am grateful for this experience, as it has taught me that if we will place our trust in the Lord, he will sustain us in our struggle with the adversary.

Filling a mission is no easy task, constantly one must seek the guidance of the spirit of the Lord, and be willing to be led by that spirit. I had to learn this great lesson (as I was carried away in the beginning) not to rely on my own knowledge. I was going to convert the whole family, how wrong I was, to think that they all were going to listen to me. No wonder I left myself open to a lot of disappointments and would become discouraged. The most important lesson I had to learn was to forget myself. It was difficult for me to understand their indifference. Yes, it was wonderful to see their son and brother after 17 years, but to be told that they were wrong in their belief was something else. Only one of my sisters out of the five had an open ear and I had the privilege to baptize her with two teenage daughters. After losing myself in the work as a missionary, I began to enjoy my work and faith promoting events strengthen my testimony.

Having left the wife, as has been so many times done before by those who were called, did not work out so well. After a few months she made preparation to come to Holland and was called to be with me to serve the last 18 months. I began to see the hand of the Lord in this move. Renting our home to two lady teachers for the time of 18 months, who paid the rent in advance was more as she needed for the trip. Everything seem to fall in its place. Our experiences on our mission has been many. Some not too pleasant which we rather forget, some very faith promoting.

AS I began to labor in Amsterdam with a young brother, it was difficult to climb those stairs to the 40th story and knocking on the door and made yourself know as a missionary and to try to make contact with people and trying to deliver the message. It was for me a big challenge and I began to admire the enthusiasm of my young partner. I can't say I ever have converted anybody to the gospel. I only hope I might have planted a seed here and there. After laboring in Amsterdam, I was transferred to Den Helder the city we lived in for eight years before we came to Zion.

My whole attitude needed to change. I began to realize I needed more knowledge, more patience, more tact, more understanding, more need of the help of the Lord, and above all, more humility.

As people have gone through the most difficult five years in the history of the nation, the suffering and privation has been so great no wonder that many lost their faith in a loving God. Unable to understand how this great war has to come over them.

As I through prayer began to change my approach to meet the people, I began to see the people as they are, not as I thought they should be, laboring as a missionary became a joy, appreciating so much more the blessing of the gospel, and desire to have others those same blessing, became my sole purpose of my labors.

The city I was to labor in, I met many who I remember I served with in the navy and made some pleasant contact with them. Naturally I was very much interested in the lives of those I used to serve with in the flying service. And must hear of the many who have lost their lives during the war.

The mentality of the people, always seem to come down to this one question "How can you expect us to forgive the enemy, after all that has been done?" Not easy to give a satisfying answer. I remember coming in contact with a lady, who told us this story. She and her husband and a 13 year daughter had kept themselves away from any kind of hate and strife. The day of liberation, they took to the street to celebrate, and a sniper bullet took the girl from between them. Could you give me an answer? Of course I could not give an answer in a few words. But if we will learn to understand the great plan of salvation, and learn that this loving child is not lost and that the plan of the Father make it possible to be reunited, that this passing from this life is not the end then that temporary separation is much easier to bear.

The welfare work of the church has brought many back to the church and many non-members began to investigate the teaching of the church and members and non-members received help as much as possible. At least many doors were opened up to present the restored gospel.

One of our treasured faith promoting experiences happen in this city. When I was still laboring with my partner, Bro. Atkins. There were about 1700 prisoners together in a prison camp who had collaborated with enemy in any kind of degree and were waiting to be sentenced. We were given permission to meet with a group of about 20-25 of these men once a week, having much success and using these men to hand out tracts, which was a thorn in the eye of the camp clergy, and this caused the permission to be canceled.

As I told these men that next week it would be the last time to be able to meet with them, and that we would use the two hours to attempt to answer all the question you men might have in mind. This would please them and they would be ready. Now there were a few of them well versed in the scripture, and during the week we prayed often for the Lord to help us to meet the challenge. As time came for our last meeting we knelt down and ask the Lord not to disappoint these men. Oh how wonderful it went, and how grateful we were for have had the spirit of the Lord to bring answers to my mind, answers which I did not know I knew myself. I still can see some of these men tears running down their faces. We were so grateful for the spirit that was manifested so distinct that meeting.

We had a sad experience. We had spent an evening with a cousin of my wife and the husband and children, who were devoted Catholic. After a pleasant evening this man being in his forties, all of a sudden passed away with a stroke. This was a shock to all of us. It was a new experience to see his wife accepting this great loss, and to witness the administration of the last rites. Also to witness all that is going on before the coffin taken to the cemetery.

After staying with him all the night hoping he would give any sign of life, yet not a single move, but breathing slowly. As the end was near, two nuns came and as they hold a burning candle and the nuns and family continually praying giving him the last rites. I was very much impressed to see how this was done, and to notice the complete self control of those nuns and the family. The absolute faith and trust they had, that this was the will of the Lord and that all would be well with them and with him. That this has to happen after a pleasant evening, a pleasant conversation about the gospel and about the work I was doing as a missionary, has me still wondering.

Those seven month I labored in this city, which is the navy base I served for eight years as a navy man, brought back many memories of the years I lived there and had wonderful experiences. Anxious to know what had become of that airfield I flew from, I found nothing but two big piles of rubble. Everything destroyed. As I stood there and let my mind go back 17 years when I left this place, (guided and directed by the Lord to the land of Zion.) Thinking about the many who lost their lives in this holocaust, which lasted only a few minutes.

As I one day walked the street and found that small building that has been used as meeting house in which we attended our first sacrament meeting. Proud and self conscious as I was, reluctant to go in such a humble building, I had to overcome my pride. But feeling the spirit which was felt. I could overlook the poor furnishing, the poor people. But was impressed by the sincerity of those two elders trying so hard to preach the truth in somewhat broken tongue. I was deeply impressed. All this come back to my mind when I stood there after being away for 17 years.

Walking few streets finding the home we used to own and taking a picture, I was reminding myself, this is the home the gospel was introduced to us. And thankful made me see the hand of the Lord. May my descendants someday appreciate the fact of us having accepting the gospel, and way has been opened to received the blessing of the gospel.

March 1948, we transferred to the branch in Haarlem. This branch was well organized, and attendance in the meeting runs 50-60 members. We rented a room above a bicycle store of the family Hengeveld. We lived there one year. As branch President I had more responsibilities than a regular missionary. Responsible for the tithing and fast offering money, and the records I was to keep up to date, yet tracting was also one of our main activities, much of it was done by bicycle, which sure kept the wife trim. This tracting was not too much of my hobby. I always had to overcome a certain resistance. The wife felt so much freer to meet the people and I admire her for it. Of course, if she made some kind of a contact, she would blow her horn to get me to take over.

Those investigator evenings I felt more to my liking. Those families usually were interested and would come up with the questions and conversation would freely flow. But making contact with people just standing in their door sometimes windy and cold or raining, seldom was a pleasure. Anyway we already were pleased if they would accept our tract hoping they would read it, as I had done 18 years ago. And I began to understand how happy those first two boys were when we began to be interested in their message, and let them come to our home. So we felt the joy to find people who wanted to know more about Mormonism, and to see them accept the teaching and to see the change taking place in their way of living and in due time see them enter the water of baptism, and to see them grow happy. This made us overlook all disappointments. The most disappointment we ever felt and could make us cry, is when some real good investigators making progress and even become members of the church, then

influenced by some enemy of the church, fall away. This indeed make one shed tears.

In this branch we celebrated our 25 year anniversary. The members making a big affair of it. We were thankful for the effort they put up to make that day a day never to be forgotten. First all to bring forth the drinks and refreshments. Times were still scarce and most things still rationed. Mrs. Henegeveld, our landlord, his hobby he loved to follow was to be in the kitchen and to cook up all kinds of nice things.

The fact that my parents and some of my brothers and sisters were coming to help celebrate our wedding day. They were very much curious how these Mormons were having a party without smoking or strong drinks. How it would be possible to have a good time. I myself was wondering how my father and brothers, being heavy smokers, would be able to get through the evening without it. The program arranged by the young people of the branch was so joyful and so pleasing to all of us, even they apparently did not even miss their smoke. And we almost were getting too late to bring on the refreshments. As my people has to get the train to go home. Later on we have heard so many fine comments about that Mormon party. They all have been taught some gospel without preaching that evening.

We were very pleased to get a call from our eldest son who was at that time in Japan. And his congratulations came over so clear as if he was standing beside us, we were so pleased with this thought fulness. Our youngest son, Bill, was at that time in the Coast Guard in Portland, Maine, and we got word from him by letter. As a family we were spread out over the globe.

As we labor to the best of our ability to keep the branch growing time was flying by. Just not time enough to do all the things I wanted to do. For example, in the city of Haarlem is the archive for the whole province of North Holland, and every hour I could spare I was gathering more genealogy of my people. This has been my hobby from the time I heard of it, and have been busy with it all the years I have been a member of the church, and have a testimony of this so important labor.

The wife and I and two young missionaries labor in that city and one Sunday those two were to prepare themselves to take up the time with their talks. I just was not prepared that day and as time came close to start the meeting the fellows did not show up I became alarmed. And as I went in a little room and knelt down to ask the Lord that nothing serious might have happen with them. I prayed for help, so the people would not be disappointed this sacrament meeting. As I open the meeting with prayer and a song I was wondering what would I now have to do. Just as we made preparation for the sacrament, President Zappy and two brethren from the office came in to visit the branch and, of course, were invited to speak.

How grateful I am the Lord always be there to answer our prayer and give spiritual food to the people of the branch.

In the year 1948, we were encouraged to start on some work project. The condition of the saints in Germany was still very poor. So much was destroyed and welfare goods from the church which has helped so many of our saints, could just not be sent to saints in that country. The priesthood bearers of the branch decided to rent a piece of land and to raise potatoes and to send them somehow to Germany. Now just imagine, here a few people who have suffered so much of the regime of the Germans, started to raise potatoes for their former enemy. We went ahead, rented, with a lot of luck, a piece of land and together we went ahead, the Lord blessing us in our effort which we can prove with this photo. This truckload has been taken by Pres. Zappy over the boundary with great difficulty in order to pass by the custom officers. Yet the Lord opened the way to get those potatoes to the members of the church in Germany, and have given us great satisfaction.

Our labors in this branch has been enjoyable and we have felt the blessing of the Lord many times.

One day it was necessary for me to give notice to the members, about some special meeting, I do not remember too well. As I got on the bike and intended to make a left hand sweep through town, suddenly I felt I should have gone to the right, which I did, and the very first home a knock on the door, The sister who was very much in distress open the door and said "Oh brother come in, my husband is dying." This was a new experience to me, but was able to call the doctor and some relative. I was so glad to be of help to this elderly sister, and to have listen to that feeling I got to change my route.

One more experience I would like to mention. One of the active families in the ward had a loss in the family. This sister lost her father who was very old, however, he was not respected by the family, his life has not been as it should have been, especially towards his elderly wife. I do not know any details, but I was called give a talk at the funeral. I was very much concerned what I could say on an occasion like this after I was informed about the life of this man. As I was sitting in the parlor waiting for the family, I sincerely prayed the Lord to direct me in what to say, and as the family came in, without planning beforehand, I open the Book of Mormon and began to read from the 34 chapter of Alma beginning 28 verse to 37 verse all about procrastination, I don't know of any affect this part of the Book of Mormon has had upon any of them only I know that the Lord directed me to it. This has been the very first time I was call to speak on a funeral.

On the eight of Feb. 1948, I had the very pleasant experience to be called to the city of Utrecht to participate in an impressive baptismal service which was held in a swimming pool of the city, which was rented for the occasion. After several children were baptized, I had the privilege to baptize my sister Annie and her two daughters, Nellie 18, and Tiny 14. This was for both of us a joy, as we were not anymore the only ones in the family. And as in due time more of her family were coming in the church. It must have had it's affect upon the rest of our family as from that time on they became more interested. But although the gospel has been preached in various ways and testimonies has been born, thus far none has joined. I remember so well the many reasons one thinks he has of not joining.

I look back to the time after investigating for more than a year, we were going to be baptized. We were with three couples, Bro. and Sis Lakerveld, Bro. and Sis Boogaard, and the wife and I. This was going to happen in the North Sea, late in the evening to prevent any disturbance or heckling. It was on a nice evening Sept. 1, 1927. The sea was fairly calm, we needed to walk quite a distance to have deep enough water as the shore is very shallow. So the members on the shore could not watch the baptism. In later years, I thought many times about that baptismal service, after attending that kind of service in the tabernacle. Sis. Boogaard, now deceased, did not dare to walk that far in the sea, but was baptized in a canal the next day.

The first time I went to church, how sensitive I was to be ridiculed or to be mocked, to be seen even by some acquaintances or friends. No I was not that type of a person that was converted in a day and then go out on the street and proclaim the gospel truths. I was too conscious of the fact of the need of greater change, as an aviator and to affiliate himself with a group of Mormons of whom no good could be spoken of. Did I not have moments to call this whole thing off? Yet something drove me on and coming in that poor little building that was used as a meeting place did not appeal to me at all. Those old ratten chairs, the smell in that place, that moisture along the walls, all this I lost sight of when those poor people began to sing "Let the lower light be burning, send a gleam across the wave; some poor fainting, struggling seaman, you may rescue; you may save." This made a deep impression upon me. Could I be that struggling seaman? (301 in song book)

Religion   My Missions

MISSION SERVED IN **Netherland.** DATES **March 1947** TO **March 1949**
MISSION PRESIDENTS **Cornelius Zappy**
I WAS SET APART BY **Steven L. Richard** DATE **March 1947**
MISSION HEADQUARTERS *(city and country)* **The Hague. Netherland.**

AREAS OF LABOR AND COMPANIONS

AREA	COMPANIONS	COMPANION'S HOME ADDRESS
Amsterdam	apr 27-1947 Br Stokes	?
Zutfen	June. 2. 1947 Br. Stokes	?
Den Helder	July 11-1947 Br Atkins	?
Den Helder	Dec 9-1947 Br Jaussie	?
Den Helder	Feb: 4-1948 Sister Dinkelman	
Haerlem	March 7-1948 " "	

In this City we served untill our release 23 March 1949.

Br Jaussie

Pres: and Sister
C. Zappy

Jast. us. two

Br Atkins

Br. Stokes

Jacoba and Hendrik as mission companions

Jacoba and Hendrik with unnamed missionary

Notice the mystery peeker in the window

Hendrik with other missionaries at the Salt Lake Mission Home March 4, 1947

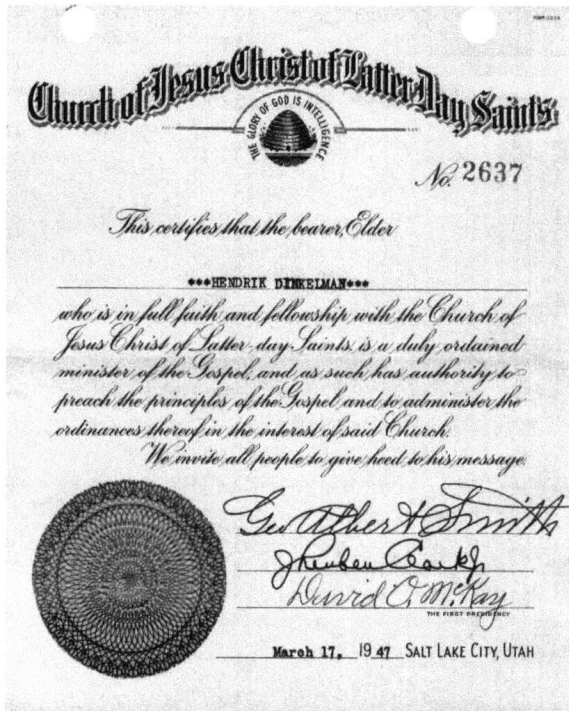

Note the signatures of this document.
George Albert Smith, J.Rueben Clark and David O. McKay

Mission Farewell Program Cover

The Saints in Holland grew potoates to help their suffering German Brothers and Sisters

Mission Journal Transcription

The following section is a transcription of the original daily mission journal kept by Hendrik while serving his mission to the Netherlands.

The original mission journal can be viewed online by entering the following into your search engine: **Church History Library Catalog, Dinkelman Family Journal, MS 35783**

[*One may notice while viewing the original journal the beginning entry indicates this journal belongs to Bill Dinkelman, as well as some entries by a young Bill. It is assumed that Hendrik took Bill's diary to use on his mission because it was not being used by his son Bill at the time.*]

[*Transcription of this journal was made without correction to spelling or grammar.*]

1947

April 4

I Hendrik Dinkelman promised myself on the day of my departure to the mission field to keep my record of the happenings during the time I leave until the time I return home, that I faithfully may keep this promise with the help of the Lord.

7:30 p.m. I left my wife who is so dear to me, and my home in Salt Lake City to fill a mission for the Church of Jesus Christ of Latter-Day Saints.

It is with joy in my heart that I am called to labor in my native country of Holland. Also with sorrow of leaving my dear wife behind, that I start on my journey.

April 5

The whole day in the train and enjoy it very much, did not sleep much because it was crowded too much.

April 6

Sunday 11 o'clock arrived at Chicago. Had a very good night, had a double chair to sleep on. Was transferred to another station and left Chicago 1 p.m. with the New York Central

April 7

Arrived in New York 7:30 a.m. Did not sleep much, too crowded. However, did enjoy the trip very much. Was very much surprised to find the train riding that smooth and fast.

After waiting a couple of hours, we were met by fam: Moen of New Jersey who are fine members of the church.

We made a fine drive through Central Park. Could not imagine the vastness of the park. Also, we made a nice drive through New York and got a idea of the greatness of that city. Then we went to the home of Br. Moen and had a very pleasant evening. Alwais be thankful to that fam. I will be.

April 8

After a very good sleep and an excellent breakfast we went on our way to Hoboken where we were to board the ship which we did in the afternoon.

We left after saying goodbye to Br. Sis Moen and thanking them for their fine hospitality. We left the shore 5 p.m. and where on our way to Holland.

Sea that evening calm.

April 9

Our first day on board – good weather. Felt like going back.

Everything too doggone classie. Just felt a little out of place. But made up mine mind not to be bothered by that feeling and I felt better after that. Food is perfect.

That evening storm coming up, did not sleep much.

Made 288 mile.

April 10

Bad storm, many sick people. I have no trouble of which I am thankful.

Made 377 mile.

April 11

Very bad weather all day. Ship is rolling bad and as me is told reached at times 35-40 degrees. Not many on the table at diner time. I feel fine. Wind and very heavy sea.

Made 330 mile. Sleep fairly good

April 12

Storm is over but a big swell which made the ship roll bad.

Made 405 mile.

Everybody need rest, walking on deck is still difficult.

April 13

Try to study and read. Walk deck a great deal and made some acquaintances.

Made 426 mile.

Picture show this night (Canyon passage)

April 14

Another day and that is all. Made 415 mile.

April 15

Still a other day. I read so much I am getting tired of it.

Made 410 mile. Passed an oil tanker.

Evenings picture show (The Killer) which I don't like.

April 16

Start looking the coast of England. Everybody start feeling good. Sea and weather are fine.

Start passing different ships which helps kill time. I start packing some of my belongings. Latest rumor is we will land tomorrow 5 p.m.

Made 404 mile.

April 17

This is a great day. I was nervous and could not sleep such. Got out of bed 4:30 and stood, after taking a shower, on deck at 5 a.m. We were in the English canal and did pass quite a few ships.

Took pilot on board at about 10 o'clock. Coming on waterway about 12 o'clock and got my first eye full of the destruction in and around the waterway. Got the ship tied up one o'clock.

The most thrilling experience of seeing 3 br. and 3 sisters on the shore. I will never forget the happy feelings which I got. Was very glad to see Jo. Wachter, also to see all the br. and sis. of the church who give us a real welcome.

Went with Br. and Sis. Zappy to the Haag and together with Jan and Adriaan that evening to Hilversum where I kissed mother at 9:30 p.m.

April 18

My impression of the familie and the conditions are much better as I expected. Have some difficulty in speaking Dutch and I feel a little ashamed. After all the excitement of coming home and staying up late I had a good night sleep.

Today I paid a visit to all the homes of br. and sis. Listened nearly all the time to all the stories of the happening during the war and during the bevijding. And I felt more than any time before how the Lord has blessed them through all these trials and how wonderful he has answered our prayers. And felt a deep thankfulness in my heart.

April 19

Today Saturday went out on the bike and visit some more friends and went with Jan to Baarn to visit Adrian and Sientje. While there I got engaged in a very fine discussion about the gospel and belief to have sow the seeds of it and in humbleness. I hope and pray that it may spout.

April 20

Sunday. Sit in the house all day wrote a letter to the wife. In the afternoon br. and sis were coming and much talking went on, which was very pleasant.

Eat bread with 12 on the table. Evening more were coming and the house was full. After talking back and vort for a while I got a opportunity to speak about the principles of the church and I felt thankful for the interest they showed.

It was a very pleasant day.

April 21

I left Hilversum for Apeldoorn to meet the folks of my wife. I arrived about ten o'clock and had a very fine welcome. Found the familie in tip top shape also the conditions.

Much is told me about the narrow escape of two bombs which fall and exploded near their home, which was damaged a great deal. However all is again brought in good shape. The house of the neighbor was wiped out and the lady of the house was kilt.

April 22

There wasn't much going on today and the day is kind of dragging.

Made a walk with Jo and see part of Apeldoorn.

April 23

Today Jo went back to Rotterdam and I went to see the old neighbor Mrs. Dykstia (or Dijkstra) 83 year old, also her daughter and husband. We had a very pleasant reunion and a very pleasant confersation. After eating with them I had a wonderful opportunity to explain in part the teachings the church, giving me their full attention. Again I hope I have sow the seed of the gospel and pray again it may sprout.

I feel very grateful.

April 24

Spent nearly all day writing a letter to the wife and bring up to date my diary and figured out my expenses which I have made so far.

April 25

Friday. My br. Adriaan came and got me with his car and brought me from Apeldoorn to Baarn, where I stayed all day. It was his 53 birthday.

Had a long and serious gospel talk with Father and two broeders.

Met nearly the whole fam: van Klingesen.

Went back to Hilversum that evening.

April 26

Saturday. This is the last day of my vacation. Making myself ready to go to Amsterdam.

Tiem Slaght and his wife did bring me with their car to Amsterdam of which I was them thankful.

That evening there was a boy scout party which I attended.

Met most of the brs. of the branch

April 27

Sunday. My first attendance of Sunday school, priesthood meeting and sacrament meeting. Did not have a chance to speak because those who were soon to depart for Zion were taking up the time.

April 28

Monday. My first day of trackting . Always have looked on this type of work as the most difficult part of my mission. I have found it takes a overwinning of oneself to pull the bell. One feel so weak and helpless. But when one meet people who are willing to listen to your utterances gave one much courage.

Went to the police to register and to get my ration stamps.

April 29

Second day of trackting. Had some very fine talks with some people.

However I find this trackting in these high building not very pleasant. Many times you are talking while people are standing on top of the stairway. But I hope I may overwin this feeling.

April 30

Went again trackting. Was again Uncle Piet and the fam. he live with. Tracking was successful. I am gaining more experience.

May 1

Today it rain. Study most port of the day. Went to American Consul to register. Went to Ryks museum for a hour.

May 2

Went out with two partners trackting had some fine talk. Weather got again bad, wet and cold. Took a fine shower.

May 3

Saturday

This is a vree day for missionaries to be used for writing enz:snz.

We had a very solemn baptism service. I had the privilege to baptized 5 persons. This was a wonderful experience to me.

Walking on Damrak at 8 p.m. All vihekles and people did stop in their track for 2 minute in honor for all those who fell during the war: it was very impressive.

May 4

Sunday. Priesthood meeting, Sunday school, testimony meeting and in the evening genealogy meeting. I was ask to open testimony meeting with prayer.

May 5

Today is national holy day, the day of liberation. Spent the day to read. Nasty and cold weather.

May 6

Went out trackting for 5 and one half hour and in the evening went to speak to investigators until 10 p.m. It was a fine day.

May 7

Had a missionary testimony meeting in the morning. Went trackting in the afternoon. In the evening went to see the doctor of Br. Boogoord. Had a fine conversation until 10 p.m. Were received very fine.

May 8

Did 4 hours trackting, had come fine conversation. In the evening went to investigators fam: Otto. Had a fine evening and felt the Lord has been with me to give a little more light to them.

May 9

Went out again trackting in one of the oldest part of the city. It is a pity how some of the people has to live.

Came home tired and a bit down hearted.

8 p.m. went with my partner Br. Stokes to a sinagoge and did watch a service although we could not understand anything. We felt like weeping with them as it did sound to us they were singing lamentations.

May 10

Stayed home until 4 o'clock. Washed a few clothes and studied as much as I can.

Went to Hilversum to fetch me some more clothes. Found Vader and Moeder in good health and had a enjoyable evening.

Because of much rain I was compelled to stay the night. Left next morning with first train to Amsterdam.

May 11

Sunday Mother's Day. Had a fairly good program. There was a big crowd. However I felt the program was too long and there was too much disturbance.

Went to eat at noon by Uncle Piet.

3:15 p.m. went to Alkmaar to speak in the meeting. Did meet Sis. & Br. Hendriks, Sis & Br. Keyzer who are old friends of my from den Helder. Hope to see them more often.

Went to see Br. Hendriks at his home and listen to all his experiences of the last 8 years, which have been terrible.

May 12

Monday morning rained and stayed in. Missionaries together had a fine discussion about the gospel.

Went trackting in the afternoon.

In the evening I went to a meeting of the Jehovas getnigen, left there with a feeling of the greatness of the task which I am connected with to preach the true gospel of Christ. I have seen the great power of Satan. But also believe that God will use the workings of Satan to destroy greater evils.

May 13

Went trackting 3 hours. Went to eat by Tan Tan. Felt kind of low.

Had a long talk with a man who was very bitter and I felt kind of sorry for him.

May 14

Went trackting with Br. Stokes, Br. Sandward, Br. Heath about 4 and one half hours. Had a fine day and contacted many people.

Went to see investigators over to Y. Had a very fine evening.

Came home late and tired.

May 15

Hemelsvaart dag. Went to Aalsmeer to see Simon and Nel. Found to my delight Vader, Moeder and also my sister's youngest daughter, Nelly, with her fiancé. Was glad to see them all and had a long conversation with all of them about de gospel. I feel the Lord is blessing me and is help me to spread the gospel.

May 16

Went trackting is the afternoon. Did not feel very good.

Went to see Br. Huydink, who has been in a prison kamp voor about 2 years.

I learn how terrible a condition did exist during war time and how easy it is for a man to receive unjust treatment.

May 17

Zaterday. Stayed home and wrote letters. We zendelinge bought some fresh fish and went ahead to fry which after trying a few times finally was successful.

Went to a show in de evening (The Keys to the Kingdom). Pretty good.

May 18

Zonday morning. Priesthood meting 9-10. Sunday school 10:30-12.

Sunday night 5-6:30, sacrament meeting. Had the privilege to speak for the first time. Spoke for a half hour about repentance.

To my great delight and to my surprise I found Annie de Wool and her husband in the audience.

May 19

Had a missionary meeting today. Had a fine lunch together. 11 missionaries.

Went to visit a fine investigator family, Hoedman.

May 20

Went trackting in the morning also in the afternoon. Spread 50 tracts.

Had a very fine gospel talk which is a reward for the effort I put in.

Went to see a investigator in the evening in the slumps of Kattenburg.

May 21

Went tracking for about 2 hours.

Went to see Aunt Anna but found out she has moved.

In the evening I went to see fam Bykstra in Tuindorp.

Had a pleasant evening.

May 22

Just making ready for the Rotterdamsche conference.

I felt weak and downhearted and found strength and peace of mind in sincere prayer. At times I feel the responsibility great and the load heavy.

Visit Sis. Ros, Sis Bakker.

May 23

First day of the conference had missionary meeting from 10-12, 2-5:30. Everyone gif his testimony.

There was a fine spirit felt all day. Blue and downhearted, don't know why.

Went up to see Jo Wachter. Talk with him for a hour, got some things straighten out. Slept with 10 of us on blankets on the stage in the church. Slept fine. Br., Sis. Hogan gave a fine breakfast.

May 24

Second day of the conference again, missionary meeting.

Heard talks from district presidents. Everybody was tense because all transfers were about to be announced. Br. Stokes and I were placed in Zutphen. Somehow a feeling satisfaction came over me. I feel the Lord be with me.

May 25

Pinkster day. Attended priesthood meeting in the Stadion Hall. Received some very timely instructions. Followed up with a general session, which was attended by 1130 people. Went with a fam. by de name of A. de Man

wieringershant. 3:00 and had a very pleasant afternoon. 5:30 went to evening meeting, 1100 people. Heard some very fine talks. Did expect to see some of my people but did not come. Lord knows best.

May 26

Today is field day. I was foolish enough to indulge in sockerball and now I can hardly walk so stiff I am. All our games came to a untimely stop on account a heavy shower.

In the evening we all saw a stage play at the Stadion Hall. Was pretty good.

May 27

Today our last day of the conference. We went on a boat ride all day, which was enjoyed by all of us. Trip went from Rotterdam, Gorinchem, Vreeswyk, Rotterdam, *B. 25*. Came back 10:30 in the evening.

May 28

Today went back to Amsterdam to make ready to go to Zutphen. Wrote a letter to the wife.

May 29

Stayed in Amsterdam.

Spent nearly all day straighten out my stamkaart enz. And did pack my luggage.

May 30

Went on the train with my partner who went straight to Zutphen while I stop in Hilversum to pack my trunk.

Went to see Anna en Laura and had very fine conversation. Also with Sienbje van den-tekom. Went to Baarn on the bike to see A and S who was going. Went back with Jan on the bike to Hilversum.

May 31

Had another pleasant day home, got my trunk on the train. Study for a couple of hours.

Paid a visit to Sis de Man Violen shaat 86, who lives now with her brother, who is also a member of the Kerk. In the evening had a pleasant conversation with some relative and neighbors.

June 1

Went to Sunday school in Hilversum. I had the privilege to serve the sacrament and to get acquanted with members.

2:30 in the afternoon I left for Apeldoorn to stay with Vader en Moeder Wachter. In the evening had a chance to speak for the first time about the gospel.

June 2

Left early for Zutphen. Got things straightened out. Got room by Wed. Noteboom at Warnsveld. Wish she was a little cleaner, but we hope by good example to improve the condition.

June 3

Stayed home. Study much that day. It is very hot, my partner is not feeling well. Went to the zuster hulp verleeming meeting en hopen to organize the Z.H.V. Br. Jong en his wife, my partner en me bore our testimonies.

Br. Jong and I administer to Br. Stokes before going to bed.

June 4

Study much and try to prepare myself for branch president. Went to see the mayor of the town and got our passports straightened out.

June 5

Study much with Br. Jong who is very good in scripture and can give me many good lessons. Received a letter from the wife which made me feel down. Wrote back and try to console her and I prayed the Lord to help her that she might receive strength to carry on.

June 6

Study every day about 3 or 4 hours, sometimes I feel my head throbbing trying to understand more. Went to Zulphen to start trackting but we were driven home by the rain before we got started.

June 7

Today is Saterday we did a lot of cleaning up around the house and back porch. We can see a little improvement in cleanliness which gave us hope.

I am a little upset because I have tomorrow my first Sunday as branch president.

June 8

Today my first Sunday and sacrament meeting as branch president. I praying for guidance. I am glad Br. de Jong is here.

I made some mistakes of which I am sorry but I hope to do better next time.

I spoke in Sunday School about 15 min. and in sacrament meeting 20 min.

June 9

Rain, rain all morning. Br. Stokes and I went out to see old members. Trying to get them back again.

We are still trying to find a better meeting place of which there is not much chance.

There is quite a little of friction of feeling between Br. Stokes and me. I am praying daily to be able to get along.

Received 2 pans from Moeder Wachter.

June 10

Study about 5 hours. Went trackting for the first time, put in 3 and one half hours.

Received two letters from the wife. I am afraid she won't take it as good as I expected. Still I don't think the tide is ripe yet for her to come. I pray the Lord to guide her.

June 11

Study again 5 hours but at times I feel I am not able to pick up knowledge as I would like to. Maybe I am getting too old to learn things. Went trackting 2 hours. We had spuds today. Br. Stokes is doing the cooking. Yesterday he had boiled dandelions.

June 12

As usual study class with Br. Jong for 2 hours. Went trackting about 2 hours.

Had a fine cottage meeting in the evening. I was leading the meeting and spoke for about 10 minutes. 14 people were there.

June 13

Study most of the day. Don't have any trackts and could not go out.

Went to town to order rubber stamps and made arrangements voor de zaal voor Jengdwerk in relief society.

June 14

Went to see Sister Palm who is sick. As we were ready to leave she ask to me to pray which I gladly did.

Went back home and did my wash: rain, rain, rain.

June 15

Br. Jong the district president is sick. Br. Stokes zalfd him and I sealed the solving. This was the first time for me sealing an anointing in Dutch.

Sunday school and sacrament meeting went by in fine spirit. This was the first Sunday I was without Br. Jong and felt satisfied. And felt the Lord has blessed me. We eat with Sis. Noteboom.

June 16

Went out looking for a place to meet. But no luck. We are very anxious to have a place of our own.

Went out trackting. But we had very little success. I prayed humbly to receive strength to go on and grow stronger in this work.

June 17

Went out trackting today put in 4 hours. It is always giving me a feeling of satisfaction after I have been out trackting. I was very tired when I come back home. Got a letter from Jo. Haven't had a letter from the wife for sometime.

June 18

Did not go out trackting. We got 4 missionaries from Arnhem paying us a visit. We eat all together, had a good time.

Went to the first Jeugd meeting, had 9 kids there and we all had a good time.

Not yet a letter from the wife.

June 19

Went trackting for a hour. Went to the Zieken hius to administer to Jong Meisje. I had let voorrecht om the zalving to bevestigen. Had een fyn Huisverga dering 13 aanwezig. Received a pahje from this with the view master.

Forgot mother's birthday. I felt terrible.

June 20

Today I received a letter from the wife. She is downhearted and disappointed as she is so anxious to come to me.

Did trackt about 1 and one half hour.

Went to a picture show in the evening orange propaganda film.

June 21

The longest day of the year and does it rain. Haven't had any summer yet, to speak of. Sit all day in the room trying to fix up reports. It nearly drives me nuts.

Anyone who want to be branch president is welcome to it.

June 22

Sunday today. Had a fine Sunday school, 12 children and 8 adults. We eat by Sis. Sholten and stayed there until time for meeting. Had a good sacrament meeting, spoke for one half hour, went back to the fam. Sholten for bread. I feel the Lord has blessed us today.

June 23

Making reports for the gemeente which gave me some headache, this is the first time. Went to eat by fam. Ottavanger, after which we went to see a old church house which was build in 1215. Study the rest of the day.

June 24

After our regular study class we went trackting for 3 hours. In the evening we went to a cottage meeting until 9:30. It was a busy day. Weather is wonderful.

June 25

Went trackting 1 and one half hour. Afternoon went to the jengd meeting. In the evening I went to the relief society. I feel kind of depressed on account of the lack of understanding and intolerance among the members. Satan is working full time.

June 26

Trackt today 3 hours. Had some very fine conversation and feel built up and strengthened. Went to a cottage meeting by fam. Scholten. Hope and pray we have been able to do some good.

June 27

After our regular study class I went trackting for about a hour. It is very hot today. Did not do much today and don't feel very satisfied about it.

June 28

Today is again a hot day. Feel like very much going swimming but being a missionary we have deprive ourself from that pleasure, so took a bath in a tub and went back to study some more.

June 29

This morning we had Sunday school. We enjoy it much. I am getting more experience in conducting meeting. I feel so much freer and have more confidence. Sacrament meeting in the evening there were only 5, but the Lord did bless us.

June 30

President Zappy and fam. paid us a visit and gave some encouragement. Did 2 hours trackting and had a long discussion with a Seventh Day Adventist. I feel very much the lack of knowledge and need to study much more. Went to investigators.

July 1

Today my first district missionary meeting. We were with ten of us. Had 2 pleasant meetings. In the afternoon went for a stroll and visit a institute for feeble minded. Evenings we went to a cottage meeting.

July 2

Stayed home all morning and study. Went to the Jenget meeting. We had 16 little ones. The work is progressing. Went in the evening to a fam. which are Seventh Day Adventist. Had a very pleasant evening. I think I learn something tonight.

July 3

Went trackting, and so far has been the most pleasant trackting. Went again in the afternoon and had a pleasant time. Had a cottage meeting this evening.

July 4

Kept quiet all day and study nearly all day. I feel the need to study so much, I even get headache at times. I wish my memory was better. But I belief I am paying now for all the smoking I have done.

July 5

Saterday, sit all day in the room and read and study. Rain.

July 6

Sunday. Went to Sunday school and testimony meeting. In the afternoon I went to Apeldoorn to speak in the meeting and I have felt the inspiration of the Lord of which I am very thankful.

July 7

Did 1 hour trackting in the morning, eat by Fam. Ottovanger. Went at 2 p.m. to Apeldoorn for Vaders very aar dag who was 75. I met the wife's brother Wim whom I haven't seen for better than 20 years. Had a pleasant time. But can't get to talk about the gospel. Maybe the time is not ryp. I went to see Rens Dyhstra. Had a very fine gospel talk with them.

July 8

Came back from Apeldoorn and went trackting for 1 hour before 12 o'clock. Got a telegram from Pres. Zappy to pack up and leave for den Helder. Wish I could stay in Zutphen a little longer.

Went to a cottage meeting in evening. Had after meeting prayer with the fam. Verbrek.

July 9

Pack my belongings in the morning, in the afternoon went to jengd meeting. We had 23 kids and had a good time.

Got my trunk on the truck and went myself to Hilversum. Got there 10:30 p.m.

July 10

Stayed home in the morning because of rain. Went to see Kolman fam. in the afternoon. Had some long talks with Gert and Jeane. In the evening went to see Jan and Jo who came home and also had a long talk with them. It was a good day.

July 11

Early on the train for den Helder, where I arrived 10:30. Felt terrible spiritually. Felt entirely lost. Went to see about another room, which we found. Den Helder does not appeal to me.

July 12

Am disappointed because my trunk has not arrived yet. Still feel terrible. Am with Br. and Sis Prins, who are the finest people you can ever meet.

Went to see Wim's wife for the first time.

July 13

First Sunday in Helder. Went to priesthood meeting, Sunday school and in the evening to sacrament meeting. I spoke for 45 minutes. I felt a little better.

July 14

6:40 on the train to Amsterdam to attend district missionary meeting. Did not like it all. Had hope to receive strength but came back disgusted. Back in Helder had a cottage meeting with 8 prisoners in Fort Erfprins. Had a good time.

July 15

Spend nearly all day running around. Police, Bevolking, distribution enz-enz.

Went to O. O. V. and decided to take a walk with the class and walk clear to Huisduinen We're very tired. Attended Z. H. V. in the afternoon.

July 16

Wrote some letters and study during afternoon. Got it in my head to take a good walk. Went to se my old airport, de Kooy, which is all rubble. I still feel very low. I pray a great deal for help. But I think I have to fight it out myself. Went at 8 p.m. to a genealogist. Was nobody there.

July 17

Haven't done any work for so far trackting goes. Feel a little better but not what it ought to be, but I will keep on praying and hope I will get out of it. The members are so swell to us here. It make me feel ashamed.

July 18

Have been walking all over town to get information about another building because it is pretty sure we are losing our meeting place. I am still struggling with myself.

July 19

Moved to another room which is better and has two separate bath. We have also outbyt with the room. I read and write about all day. I have a cold between the shoulder blades which gave me much trouble.

July 20

Went to priesthood meeting, Sunday school and sacrament meeting. Attendance fairly good.

I am worried so much about the feelings I have toward my work which I cannot understand.

July 21

My first day trackting in den Helder. I prayed fervently and as I put 4 and one half hours this day and had many fine conversations. I felt better as I have done for a long time. Went to Fort Erfprino but had not much success. After that I stop in by Wim to say goodbye for he is going on a 5 month cruise.

July 22

Trackt today 3 and one half hours. Br. Sandwaard was with us. Have been looking around for another vergerder place, but it is really a problem. Trust the Lord will open the way.

July 23

Me and my partner Br. Atkins are not feeling so well. We trackt 2 hours . Weather very sultry. Stayed home afternoon and prepare a talk for tomorrow night. Spent 2 hours with investigators. Had a good time. Had a fine gospel talk with Sis. Nelly.

July 24

Today nerdenking Pionier feest. I trackt 4 and one half hours, had some very fine talk.

Saw an investigator and had a very fine conversation.

Had a special meeting today. Spoke about 20 minutes.

July 25

We trackt 4 and one half hours had two fam. who called us in and spoke to them for 45 min.

Received a letter from the wife which made me feel glad. She still like to help me, but I can't see it. I hope she keep herself busy and try to overcome that lonesome feeling.

July 26

For the first time I trackt on Saturday. Put in 2 hours. This week has been a record.

I went for a long walk all along the buiten haven. Sometime it is hard to realize that I have been away 17 years. Did meet one of the old gang from the Kooy Bommazuin.

July 27

Sunday. Attended priesthood meeting Sunday school, sacrament meeting. Spoke a good half hour. Had a enjoyable day. It is plenty warm.

July 28

Went trackting. Wrote some letters. Did have not much ambition. Went in the evening to Fort Erfprins and had a good time.

We have two members who are elders and there were 9 investigators.

July 29

Wrote a long letter to the wife, which take all forenoon. Trackt in the afternoon about 2 hours.

Went to mutual. Had a very good time. I feel weak and I need the help the Lord every hour.

July 30

Trackt about 2 hours. Got myself a haircut and made preparations for the centennial in Amsterdam.

Wrote a good sized letter Nick Cannon.

July 31

Went on the train for Amsterdam went from there to Aalsmeer, where I met vader and mother. I had a very pleasant day. Did a little vissching and went back 10 p.m.

August 1

Went back to Aalsmeer and vish and came to a little rest. I had a serious talk with Nelly about the spirit in her home which is about to the breaking point. I hope and pray my talk and advice might do a little good.

Met Anna, Sona and their two daughters at the meeting house while the play (It Shall Keep Thee) was put on. It made me happy

to see them there. I pray the Lord with bless them.

August 2

Missionary meeting from 9 till 12:30 and from 2:30 till 5:30. Apostle Sonne is with us. In the evening we had a very beautiful pioneer feast in Krasnapolsky. It was very nice. Anna and Sona and 3 daughters and son in-law were there, who were all impressed with what they have seen.

August 3

From 10 to 12 conference meeting in Krasnapolsky, which was well attended. In the afternoon I felt to go to Hilversum and I visited Jur and Jeane Rinns and Aunt. Went back to Amsterdam in the evening.

August 4

9 o clock came to together by central station to start the boat ride from Amsterdam to Marken to Monnickendam and Volendam, from there back to Amsterdam by train. It was very nice day and we did enjoy it very much.. I wish I could feel spiritually a little better. 4 months ago I left SL City.

August 5

Went back to den Helder 10:30 AM, found 4 letters which made me feel a lot better. Because of rain I spend the day answering those letters.

August 6

Rain, rain all day and stayed in and studied and read. Received a letter from Boogaard. I am going to visit some of his old friends.

August 7

Went trackting 2 hours in the morning and 1 hour in the afternoon. Try to visit some investigators in the evening. Stayed by Tom Prins until 10 p.m.

August 8

Went to town, took a shower, did some trackting in the afternoon. But I just did not have the spirit. Sometimes I have much trouble and had to force myself to go out. I have not overcome my false pride to the extent that I am able to preach the gospel freely in all circumstance.

Had a very fine evening by the Jehovah's getuige. Had a good opportunity to explain some of our principles.

August 9

Made a wandering all along the buitenhaven and Binnenhaven. I like to do that once in a while on our free day. Went with Br. Prins to the dunes and looked over the bunker the Germans made during he war. Came home tired. Had a fine chance to talk gospel with relatives of Sis. Franke.

August 10

Went to priesthood meeting, Sunday School, testimony meeting and evening meeting. The day past by in a hurry. We had a fine day and were thankful to the Lord.

I eat lots of pone by Br. and Sis. Kwast.

August 11

Trackt 2 hours. Spent 2 hours making connections in an effort to line things up for a new building. Seen some of Boogaart friends and met some fine contact.

Went to Fort Erfprins to preach, had 17 investigators. And I feel the Lord is blessing us greatly in this work and I pray he will lead me continually.

August 12

7:20 a.m. went to Zutphen to get my permit for my bicycle. Got there at 1:45. Went and stayed in Apeldoorn that night, found everything OK. Jo is getting better. Had for once a gospel talk with Jo. Father had a boril.

August 13

Left Apeldoorn for Helder where I arrived 2:30. Went to see about a bike which I am about to buy. Went to see diverse member and met some fine contact again.

Spent the evening the evening talking gospel with one of Boogs friends.

August 14

Went out and spent a good bit of time looking for a bike, which I finally bought for 141.50 complete. Am kind of happy with and hope I will use it a lot.

Went to see Jo Ekkes for the first time. Was received very nice. (eat a nice vish.)

August 15

Trackt for a couple of hours but not much success. Weather is very hot. Visit a few more friend of Boog. Had some splendid talks.

August 16

Went out 5 o clock for a ride on my new bike for a couple of hours, enjoy it very much. Went home and study and took again a long ride.

Went to pay a visit by van Brummelen, had a very fine time and a fine chance to explain the gospel.

August 17

Priesthood, Sunday school and sacrament meeting. It is very warm weather. Sometimes I feel the burden quite heavy as I have to speak nearly all the time, and I feel the lack of knowledge. But the Lord has blessed me and pray he will continue to do so.

August 18

Went to Amsterdam for missionary meeting, had a good time. Coming back, went to Fort Erfprins and had a fine meeting with 23 men. The biggest so far, feel like we are doing some good.

August 19

Did about two hours trackting, met little success, feel not in tune with the work. Has some feeling towards my partner. I wish I was the wisest and let things not get a hold on me as it sometimes do. Had a cottage meeting by Kiesling, present 10 people.

August 20

Did not feel like trackting. Wrote Bishop a letter and read biggest part of the day.

Went to see the son of Sis. Keiger, had a nice evening.

August 21

Trackt 3 hours today, had some very fine talks. Spend the evening with the Erkelens.

Eat by Kloosterman and met her mother and spoke much about the gospel.

Coming back in the evening, I met some relatives of Sis. Franke and spoke again with much zeal. I feel the Lord is guiding me so often when I am to speak or explain.

August 22

Spend all morning to see notoris and trying to find out more about getting a piece of ground for a new church. Hope the Lord will bless us.

Tract in the afternoon and found a fine fam. where we were invited to come back. Visit the fam. Boon in the evening.

August 23

Went vishing 5:30 a.m in the fort gracht, got 3 nice ones. Took the bike and rode around a bit.

Went to see the fam. I found the day before and had a wonderful evening. A.v.d. Wyn Symish to met van Brummelen for a while.

August 24

Priesthood meeting, Sunday school, eat by Br. and Sis Kwast, back to the room and prepare for the evening meeting. Had sacrament meeting, very fine spirit. Stayed by Kwast during the evening. Had a gospel discussion with some of their visitors.

August 25

Trackt 2 hours in the morning. Found a lady I spoke with for one half hour, invited me to come back as soon as I could.

Seen Br. Stam who brought in boxes with clothes to be given away.

Went to Erprins had a fine meeting, several discussion with different men. 15 men in attendance.

August 26

Trackt 3 hours today. In the evening the members of the branch came together to celebrate the 40 years anniversary of Br. and Sis Kwast. There were present about 30 people. Br. and Sis Montfrans came over from Hilversum. Evening was successful.

August 27

Trackt 2 hours. It is very warm every day, and during this month there are so many people not home. Went with Br. and Sis Montfrans for a walk to this dinner and over the dyk back. Visit the Wind fam. in the evening, but not much chance to preach.

August 28

Trackt again 2 hours it is still warm but not bad. Got Br. Stam from the train and assisted him in the afternoon in distributing clothing. In the evening we had a cottage meeting in the church. Br. Stam spoke about the welfare. 20 present 2 onderzoekers.

August 29

Went out and trackt 2 hours. Received a letter from John in which he poured his heart out about his troubles. I wrote back right away, hope I have given him something what did help him on his way. Stayed home evening.

August 30

Saturday went to Texel to se the Ruins of de Mok of which I took a few pictures. Eat by Br. and Sis. Prins and spent the rest of the evening by van Brummelen. Did not speak about the gospel of which I did not feel right.

Received a letter from Bill. All is well with him.

August 31

Priesthood very ordinary. Sunday school, attendance fairly good. Went to sacrament meeting, spoke about 10 min. I am struggling for quite some time with myself, even to the extent I am losing my rest. It seems like I am standing against a wall and feel like am losing the spirit of mission. It worries me terribly, and I feel spiritually sick.

September 1

Today Queen's birthday celebration, nothing doing, just stayed home. Went to Fort Erfprins and talk to 8 men, there was a fine spirit. I spoke about organization of the church and about the word of wisdom.

Br. Atkins and I have both a bike, which saves us much walking.

September 2

Trackt this morning 2 and one half hours. I felt pretty good. It always makes a person feel good when he does his duty. Studied a couple of hours in the afternoon.

I received a package from the wife also a letter from her and from John.

Tonight our first O.O.V. We sang many fine songs and made preparation the great opening.

September 3

Went 4 and one half hours trackting. Eat by Erkelens. Went to investigators in the evening, Fam. Keyzer.

September 4

Trackt 2 hours, found a very interested fam. Hope they will become investigators. Spent the evening by fam. Prins.

September 5

Went to see Oon Jaap who has to go the hospital, visit him again in the afternoon.

Trackt for about one hour, no success at all.

Spent the evening by investigator, a good friend of Br. Vlam. Made a nice little trip on the bike to Ewyksluis.

September 6

Left this morning on the bike to schagen to see fam. Snel. Very nice road and weather. Rode up and down about 50 km. Stayed home evening because it was fast day.

September 7

Sunday school, priesthood and fast meeting in the morning and evening meeting at 5 o'clock. Spent the evening by fam. Endjes. Did not speak at the meeting.

September 8

Track 3 and one half hour. Weather is om geslagen krygen nei weer regen.

Had a very fine meeting in Fort Erfprins, 19 in attendance. Spoke mainly over the welfare. Visit Br. Kwast in Ziekenhuis.

September 9

Went out trackting 1 and one half hour. Visit some investigators to invite them for our conference. Went to the O.O.V. and spoke with an investigator. Hope he may receive the truth.

September 10

Trackt today 2 and one half hours. I felt we were successful. Had quite a few fine conversations. Received a letter from Coos *(Jacoba)* who is with Bill in New York. I hope she will settle down. Had a cottage meeting by Sis. Kloostenman, 6 persons were there.

September 11

Trackt 2 and one half hours. Visit old Sister Beyer. Received a package from home plus a letter from New York. Spent evening by Prins.

September 12

Trackt 2 and one half hours. Went to see Br. Kwast who have to be operated on. We administer to him. Which made him feel more calmer. I feel of myself weak when called upon to perform a duty like that. Yet I feel the Lord blessed me every time I am called.

September 13

This morning I received a letter from the wife telling me that she has left New York for Holland on the 12 September. A feeling of disappointment came over me and I felt like the bottom was dropping from under me. All my hopes, all my plans fell on pieces. I prayed earnestly that I may see why. I feel myself sinking. May the Lord help me.

September 14

Today Branch Conference. Spent all together 7 hours in diverse meetings. I eat by Mr. Bois who is a visherman and a very good friend of us. Spent evening by Entjes, had an enjoyable evening.

I feel better about the wife coming. I feel the Lord has taken that dark feeling away from me.

September 15 Mother's birthday

Br. Landwaard and Br Lievert stayed with us today. We went to the Mayor to talk about our building problem. We were received very friendly and we received some sound advice.

Br. Landwaard went with me to Fort Erfprins to speak to N. S. Brs.

September 16 Sena's birthday

Today I went to Amsterdam to meet with the district missionaries. Had two good meetings. Went to Hilversum for a couple of hours to see the folks. Went back to Helder same evening.

September 17

Track 4 hours today, feel pretty good about it. Went to see Br. Kwast who has been operated

on. He is a pretty sick man. We all pray he may recover soon.

September 18

Stayed home in the morning. Received 6 boxes from the welfare and spent afternoon bringing around the clothes for the members, some of whom never attend church. Spent the evening by Steyn. Had little chance to speak about the gospel. I feel down hearted.

September 19

I am alone today, took a bath, went trackting about 2 hours. Pack suitcase to send home. Went to see investigators but no success. Spent some time by Prins.

September 20

We made a bicycle trip to east end of wieringen which is 27 km from den Helder. Too bad we had such a strong headwind coming back. In the evening we tried to spend some time by investigators but it was the wrong time.

September 21

Sunday as usual, priesthood meeting, Sunday school and sacrament meeting. I spoke 30 min and I felt the Lord did guide me. Br. Kwast is doing fine and I Hope he may again completely recover.

September 22

Left Helder for Haag to see Pres. Sappy and see the welfare storehouse. Left in the afternoon for Rotterdam where I met Jo and Gert mienwehuis where I stayed for the night. Went out to see Br. and Sis Hoggan who is transferred to Amsterdam. Had a pleasant evening by Jo and Gert.

September 23

Went with Jo to see Rotterdam. We walk to the old plantage to see the destruction of the old town. I eat by Gert and we got a big schol. By four o'clock we went to see the Westerdam come in. After a pleasant voyage the wife got off the boat by 5:30. She was greeted by Jo and Tents Anna, Jaan, Sien and Marie. We were brought to Apeldoorn with a truck, where we arrived at 11 o'clock.

September 24

I feel not very pleasant, too many thing go through my mind. I see so many difficulties ahead which are weighing me down. It is all so different as I did hope for.

September 25

I spent most of my day reading. We eat by Lena. A very nice dinner. Went to a meeting and was happy to see so many acquaintances and friends.

September 26

Sit Home nearly all day and read a book. Went to visit Bockmeg and Bruervronne Dykstra. We had a very fine evening. I am feeling better now about the wife coming to Holland. I hope everything is coming out alright.

September 27

Adriaan took us from Apeldoorn to Hilversum where we arrived at 10:30 After meeting with

Voder and Mother, we went to see some of the fam. Paid a visit in the evening to my Brother Frek, who's daughter has her birthday.

September 28

Went with the wife to Sunday school in Hilversum. We were glad to see Anna, Sena and daughter there and we pray they may go on. I went in the evening to the meeting and I had the privilege to speak for about 20 min. I also had a very good chance to speak up home that evening of which I am thankful.

September 29

Stayed home during the day. Went to see Ans, Sis Jeare, and spent the evening by Jan and Jo.

September 30

Went to Amsterdam with the wife to se Oom Piet, who happen to be at the Haag. Went to Nell and Simon and spent there the day. I took the train to Helder and the wife to Hilversum. I am kind worried how she is going to keep herself occupied.

October 1

Spent part of the day unpacking some stuff which was send from SLC, found lots of stuff broken up. I did fill a suitcase and sent it to Hilversum. Wrote a letter to John and Bill, spent the evening with investigators.

October 2

Went trackting for two hours. Spent afternoon with study, and was with van Brummelen at evening. Had a very good opportunity to explain some of the principles of the gospel. My partner is not yet back from Alkman.

October 3

Trackt today 4 hours, took a bath, received a letter from Cannon (Granger). Had our opening evening O.O.V. which was successful, although I could have better organized. I took part in a lottery of which I felt not good afterward.

October 4

Today I am 6 months from home, it seems such a long time. I wrote a letter to a man on the plant. This is the first one I wrote to him. I am not feeling quite right and pray the Lord to help me to serve him better.

October 5

Today vast Sunday and as usual attended priesthood, Sunday school, vast meeting and evening meeting which was a O.O.V. We were surprised to see Br. and Sis. Zappy come in just for the meeting started. He spoke for 30 min.

October 6

We trackt to day 3 and one half hours, had some good conversations. Went to Fort Erfprins where we had a fine meeting, 13 men attended.

October 7

Trackt about 3 hours today. We are having such a beautiful weather for so long which is exceptional for this country.

Went to the O.O.V. and had a very fine evening.

October 8

Trackt today 4 and one half hours, had some very fine conversations. Spent the evening by Br. and Sis. Kwost. Br. Kwost come back home from the hospital and is now recuperating. His recovery has been remarkably fast.

October 9

Trackt 2 hours today. Spent the evening by investigators Rollstieverts of a Hamish. I wrote a couple of letters.

October 10

Took a bath in the morning. Stayed home until 3 p.m.. Took the bike and took a trip to Callandsoog, enjoy the trip very much. Spent the evening by fam. Keyzer. Did not have much opportunity to talk about the gospel.

October 11

I went to the harbor a couple of times today and spent the rest of the day reading. We eat by Prins in the evening and spent some time there.

October 12

Sunday today. Went to priesthood and Sunday school. I had the lead at sacrament meeting and I spoke for 40 min. I felt inspired. I had a very fine opportunity to explain the principles of the gospel to two sisters of Sis. Franke.

October 13

Went trackting out in the country for 3 and one half hours. We went on our bikes and had a good day. Went to Fort Erfprins and to our sorrow we are not allowed anymore to meet with the men. It makes me feel bad because it is just there where I felt we were doing some good.

October 14

I felt down all day, did not feel like going out and stayed home all day and spent time for study and reading. Went to O.O.V. in the evening. Slept bad at night. Received a nice letter and pictures from John.

October 15

Went to the church to do some work. Went trackting in the afternoon for 3 hours and had a very fine time and some nice conversations. Spent evening by fam. Jansen, had a good evening with good opportunity to explain the principles of the gospel. Wrote a long letter to John.

October 16

Haven't done any trackting today, raining and not much ambition. I read and studied as much as my poor head would let me. Spent evening by de Wyn who are investigating our teachings. Haven't heard of the wife for a week.

October 17

It rain biggest part of the day. Took a bath, clean up the church. Spent evening by Endjer.

October 18

Today is Saturday, went for a little ride on the bike.

Studied nearly all day. Went to Brummelen to spend the evening, had a fine evening.

October 19

Priesthood and Sunday school, sacrament meeting of which I had to preside over. I spoke about 20 minutes.

We eat by Br. and Sis. Kwost where we spent some time in the evening.

I am feeling low and hope there might come a change. I am praying for it.

October 20

We tract 3 hours today and had some fine conversations. Also we had a fine gospel talk with Sa v/a Hoeven and Buiteloor.

Went to investigators in the evening and had a good time.

October 21

Went to see the mayor but have to come back. Went trackting but not very successful. Did see the mayor in the afternoon and spoke about our meeting hall. Did not solve the problem we have on our hands. Hope the Lord will guide us in our search for another meeting place.

October 22

Went to work to find us a other meeting place, which I hope I found in the pastorie of the Nederduetch Hervormel church on the West-straat. Went to see the different people about our problem.

October 23

We tract about 3 and one half hours today had some fine conversations.

We were able to rent a place to meet in, it will solve least temporary our problem. Hope it all work out alright.

October 24

Today the wife came to den Helder to stay some time. Went to visit some fam. with her. Made a long walk with her. It had turned real cold, am not used to it yet. Went to a church meeting of the vryzinnige.

October 25

Spent all day visiting members it is still cold, went to see Foet and Jo Ekkes.

October 26

Sunday as usual 3 meetings, the wife attended Sunday school and sacrament meeting, she spoke for a few minutes.

October 27

Spent the day with the wife we visit some Sis. and Br. Spent the evening by van Brummelen. Had a nice evening.

October 28

Spent this day also with the wife went to mutual in the evening.

October 29

Not doing much today. Spent some time with Erkelens. The wife is visiting fam. Ekks. I went

there in the evening. Mr. Ekkes got a blood-starting in the brain which left him half lame. I sat on his bed all night.

October 30

Spent all day by the fam. Ekkes. The man is getting worse and there is no hope for his recovery. The wife and I try to help wherever we can.

October 31

This morning 5 o'clock Mr. Ekkes past away. This was for me and the wife a new experience, which made us realize how much we have as LDS compared by others.

We moved to a new location with our branch. I am thankful the Lord opened the way and hope and pray we might in time get our own building.

November 1

Sent some time with the wife. Did a little work in the branch. Did a great deal of reading and went to bed early.

November 2

Sunday. Priesthood, testimony meeting, 5 o'clock meeting. I spoke 35 minutes. Went to visit some investigators.

November 3

Attended the funeral of Rimus Ekkers, first in the church and then on the graveyard. Spent the evening by Toets and relatives.

I am very much troubled about myself and about my wife. Things are not going right – I hope and pray the Lord will help us to solve our difficulties.

November 4

Tract 2 and one half hours and had some fine conversations.

Went with the wife to visit fam. Stein. Had a good evening.

November 5

Received a letter from Madill. I wrote them back right away. Spent reading all morning.

Went to primary to see how they make out in our new location.

I am not feeling well, don't know what is the matter.

November 6

Went tracting for about 3 and one half hours. Spent evening visiting fam. with the wife, who is still with Jo Ekkers.

November 7

Took a bath this morning. Spent morning studying and reading. Went to O.O.V. in the evening.

November 8 Vader's birthday.

Went with the wife to Hilversum where we celebrated Father's birthday who is 80 years today. We had a very fine evening. There were 65 people present.

November 9

Today we had district conference. There were many members all meetings. I spoke for about 15 min. during the evening meeting. Went back to Hilversum and stayed by Jeane and Jan.

November 10

Spent the morning with Jean and talk about the gospel all morning. Went to Father and Mother and visit Trits who is sick Evening went back to Helder.

November 11

Rain pretty near all day. Study as much as I can. Wrote a letter to John

November 12

Went to Amsterdam for a branch president meeting where we are instructed to look for prospect for local missionaries.

November 13

Bad weather all day, sit in the room and study and read till my head get sore. I am feeling low.

November 14

I take a bath and stay pretty near home all day and study as much as I can.

Went to O.O.V. in the evening.

Wish I heard some from Bill

November 15

Rain and some more rain. Went to Fort Erfprins. Try to see Br. Falkeburg but could not get in touch with him.

I am fasting today as I feel I have to try to whip myself in line of my missionary work. I am not having the spirit.

November 16

Priesthood meeting and Sunday school, it is stormy weather but still a good attendance. We had Br. and Sis Stam with us at the sacrament meeting in which they occupy the time. Haven't heard from Bill yet.

November 17

Started today on the church wide counting of the members. I am kind of glad because it gives a change in the work of us missionaries. I am sleeping very bad. It worries me. I am always hoping that something will happen.

November 18

Spent some hours with recording members. Not much doing the rest of the day.

November 19

We kept on going today to gather more information for the church census.

November 20

We spent more time to complete the church census.

November 21 Wife's birthday

I went to see today the fam. Snieder who are living way out in the country. I walk many km today. We had a pleasant time. I walk from Burgerburg to Enigenburg and then from there to Burgervlatburg and visit fam. van Ee.

November 22

Rain. Rain. Went to see Toet and fam. Spent a pleasant hour and talked about the gospel. They showed much interest.

November 23

Sunday school, priesthood meeting and sacrament meeting. There was a fine spirit in the evening meeting. Spent the evening by investigators, and we had a wonderful evening. Haven't heard from Bill yet.

November 24

Rain. Bad weather. Study and read. Wrote a couple of letters. Went to investigators that evening.

November 25

We tract about a hour. It is cold today. Nasty weather. Went to Adema fam. that evening.

November 26

Cold weather. Study most of the day. I am reading very fine book about the pyramids of Egypt. Went to see the Allen fam.

November 27

I went to Amsterdam for a district missionary meeting. We had a very fine testimony meeting and after that there was a very fine Thanksgiving dinner prepared for us by Sis. Stam and Vernei. I stayed on the way back in schagen for a hour to see Br. Hubert

November 28

I tract 2 hours today. It is plenty cold and I am seeing up against the winter. Went to the O.O.V. in the evening. I haven't heard from Bill for such a long time. I am worrying a bit.

November 29

Bad weather. I paid a visit to fam. v. Brummelen. Studied biggest part of the day. Went to investigators Bregmon.

November 30

We had today with us Br. Vlam who spoke on the evening meeting. We spent a fine day and enjoyed the spirit of the Lord. We had a splendid time by fam. Endjes.

December 1

It is cold and nasty – spent about 3 hours by Bintelaar. Wrote a letter to Bill. I was very glad to receive a letter from him this morning. Went to investigators during the evening. I am reading a book about the great pyramid, very interesting.

December 2

Received a letter from the Madill. Tract 2 and one half hour, had some fine conversations. The wife came to den Helder to see Vim. Spent the evening by v. Brummelen.

December 3

Went to Winkel to see Br. and Sis. Vlam. The wife was with me. We had a pleasant visit although the weather was bad. Spent the evening by the fam. Allen.

December 4

Tract one hour. It is awfully cold and nasty. Went to see investigators. The wife is in town to see her brother. Did go to see her.

December 5

Took a bath. Today is Saint Nicolaas day. Again went to see the wife. Spent some time talking with Vim.

December 6

Made a long walk with the wife, and we spoke very serious about our spiritual condition and our future. I am losing much sleep and feel my nerves on edge all the time. Spent the evening by Vim, who showed us his films

December 7

Sunday today. Went to 4 meetings. Did not see the wife today. I feel low and pray the Lord to lead me through our difficulties.

December 8

Spent some 4 hours with investigators.

December 9

Received word from Pres. Sappy this morning, my partner will be transferred to Utrecht. I went trackting 2 and one half hours and had some splendid conversations. I had a busy day and feel greatly blessed.

Spent the evening by fam.Schutle, who has lived in S.L. City a number of years.

December 10

Tract one hour. Spent 4 hours with investigators, had a splendid evening. Visit Sis. Kwast who is sick. Have been very busy again today.

December 11

Today my new partner came in so I have a privilege to break him in. His name is Janssie. We eat by Sis. Ewald. Try to visit some investigator. I bought some nice flowers for our 24 anniversary.

December 12 24 years married.

First I took a shower, then I got Bro. Janssie fix up for his distribution, his passport and county recorder.

Spent 2 and one half hours by a new investigator. Went to see Sis. Kwast who is sick. Spent the evening by fam. Keyzer. Saw the wife a short while.

December 13

Kept busy all day with diverse things. Went to see the sick and to see some friends.

December 14

Sunday. Went to different meetings. Spoke about 20 min. about gathering. Felt a little disappointed about my wife who is in town did not come to meeting.

Spent the evening by fam. Prins. It was his birthday.

December 15

Study most of the morning. Went to see investigators. Was not very successful. Spent evening by Bro. Kelens. Had a good evening. I slept very good this night.

December 16

Went tracting about 2 hours. Spent about 4 hour investigators. Had a very nice evening. Had a very busy day. I received a nice letter from Ruel Paul of which I am very pleased

December 17

I tract about one hour. Spent some time by van Brummelen and spent the evening by fam Allen.

December 18

We tract 1 and one half hour. Visit come fam. Spent the evening by Seienaar. Wrote some letters. Received a nice letter from Ruel Paul.

December 19

Rain. Rain. Study most of the day. Took a bath. Wrote a letter. Went to the O.O.V.

December 20

Saw the wife for the short while visit the sick. Spent 2 and one half hours by fam. de Wyn. Had a splendid evening.

December 21

3 meetings today. We eat by fam. Kwast, and stayed there all afternoon. We had a splendid

sacrament meeting. There were six investigators. We felt greatly blessed.

Brought the wife back home and stayed there to talk with Vim and his family.

December 22

Did all kind of things today, some shopping, etc. Spent the evening by fam. Burgers. Time was well spent.

December 23

Monkey around about all day. Try to spend some time by investigators, but not much luck.

December 24

Went to Amsterdam with the wife and my partner to attend a district missionary meeting and a Kerstfast dinner. Came back by 7:30 p.m. and spent the evening by Vim and Toet.

December 25

Christmas day. Study with my partner the Dutch language. Had a fairly good Christmas party in the afternoon.

Spent the evening by fam. Prins.

December 26

I worked an hour to straighten out our meeting place.

Spent a couple of hours by van Brummelen, had a fine time. Had a very fine evening party.

December 27

Rained nearly all day. Went to the hospital to visit the sick. Got myself soaked wet.

Spent the evening by investigators Wiedema.

December 28

Sunday, last meeting of the year. Attended 3 meetings spoke about 40 min.

Spent the evening by fam. Stein.

December 29

Spent most of the day making preparations for my short vacation.

Br. and Sis. Sappy came to see me to give me authority to look for building ground. Went to see Vim and his fam. in the evening;

December 30

Went to Hilversum with the first train. Coming home I spent all day by Anna who had her birthday. Had a very fine day.

December 31

Spent the afternoon in Baarn to see Adriaan and Sien.

He has been laying in bed for a couple of weeks. Wife, me, father, mother spent the last evening of the year by Jeane and Jur. Had a good time.

1948

January 1

Spent the day home by Vader, Moeder. Nearly all the family came to bring in their best wishes.

Spent the evening by Jan and Jo. Had a very fine chance to explain the gospel. It was very late when we left.

January 2

Went back to Helder after picking up my partner in Amsterdam. Arrived in Helder at 6:30. Went to O.O.V. that evening. I am much troubled with headache.

January 3

Saturday today. I took a bath, studied and went to the hospital to visit the sick. I am not feeling right.

January 4

Attended 4 meetings today. Spoke 45 min. during evening meeting. Spent the evening by fam Allen.

January 5

I am spending time looking for ground for building. Spent afternoon by Burgers and the evening by de Wyn, had a fine day. I wrote some letters. Received a package food from headquarters.

January 6

Went to see Mr. Howath who is city architect. It seems like it will be a long time before we will see our new building. Spent the evening by Leienaar. I received a letter from the wife. I am in a downhearted mood. I think it must be the weather.

January 7

Bad weather. Stayed in all morning and studied. Spent the evening by Keyzer.

January 8

Not feeling right. It is very stormy weather. Received a letter from Vader Wachter giving me his side of disharmony between the wife and home. I am feeling worried.

Spent the evening by Sheurleer. Had a good evening.

January 9

I am not feeling good yet. Wrote a letter back to Jo. I received one from him this morning, giving me his view about the trouble. Wrote a letter to the wife. Paid a visit to the hospital. Went to the O.O.V.

January 10

Our free day. Made a long walk along the dyk. Stayed in Beth until noon because I am not feeling so well.

January 11

Attended 4 meetings today. I went to fam Kwast and stayed all afternoon.

Weather was very bad.

January 12

I feel sick. Weather is bad. Paid a visit by van Brummelen. Had a fine evening. Coming home I found 3 letters which made me feel better.

January 13

Studied a little and wrote a letter.

Spent 5 hours with investigators. Had good day.

January 14

Spent some time in trying to find more information about ground.

Run around a great deal to try to make contact with investigators.

Spent the evening by Roll Sievert but I felt not satisfied.

I am feeling better and am sleeping better. Got two packages, one from Boog, one from Elder Guorrem. I am pleased

January 15

Wrote a letter to Boogaard to thank him for his package.

Spent evening by Keyzer.

Try to see some investigators but not much success.

Went to fort Erfprins to see the minister. I will try again.

January 16

Spent a couple of hours looking for ground for building.

Spent the evening O.O.V. Paid a short visit by Toets.

January 17

Spent 3 hours looking for ground and addresses.

Went to fort Erfprins to see some prisoners, which finally happen.

January 18

Sunday, as usually went to 3 meetings and spoke for about 40 min. Spent some time making reports by Prins.

January 19

Spent again 3 hours looking for ground. Spent the evening by a old friend, v. Beveren, had a fine evening.

Went to see Oma for her birthday.

January 20

Received a letter from the wife. Spent 5 hours with investigators. Had very fine evening by fam v. d Hoek.

Wrote some letters today.

January 21

Spent again 5 hours with investigators. Had a good day and felt blessed.

Haven't heard from the boys for a long time.

January 22

Did a little tracting today. I am not doing much. Sometimes I feel like going on a vacation. Winter has been wonderful so far.

January 23 My birthday.

Today a year ago I got my call for my mission, and today I got a letter from the wife telling of her call and I belief the Lord know what is good for us. And I hope and pray that we will have his spirit to guide and lead us.

Went to O.O.V. today. Got a letter from Bill. I am glad.

January 24

Wrote back to Bill spent some time finding a solution about our meeting house. It is cold today. Spent the evening by Prins.

January 25

Regular Sunday meetings. Eat fish by Br. and Sis Kwast, very delicious. Had a fine fireside chat by Prins.

January 26

Spent all afternoon by Brummelen and spent a fine evening by Leienaan, had a good opportunity to preach the gospel there.

January 27

Received a letter from Boogaard. Spent 5 and one half hours with investigators.

January 28

Visit some saints and did some business.
    Wrote a letter to the wife and received one from Pres. Zappy.

January 29

Spent 5 hours by investigators. We eat by van Brummelen. Spent evening by Keyzer.
    I am not feeling satisfied. Went to see the head of the weder op bouw.

January 30

Went to Amsterdam district meeting. Had a very good meeting. President Zappy was with us and gave us some very timely instruction.

Had a welfare meeting in the evening to prepare the members for our welfare project.

January 31

Took a trip to Huisduinen and went up the light house and walk along the shore.
    Spent a couple of hours by Leienaan. It was fast day.

February 1

Regular Sunday. Br. and Sis. Stam came for a visit. We had a good testimony meeting. Spent the evening by a new investigator. Luidinga.

February 2

Try to get in touch with the main of free, but no luck. Waiting for a letter which supposed to be here a couple of days ago. Spent the evening by Woord.

February 3

Send a telegram to Pres. Zappy, but no answer.
    Br. Stam came during the evening to visit investigator Bondt.

February 4

Did go to den Haag to set apart my wife who is called on a mission. Came back early and went to see fam. Keyzer.

February 5

Spent some time checking out Br. Janssy.
    Went to see fam. Wachter. Vader made ready to go to Hilversum.

February 6

Took the 9:10 train to Hilversum. Stop in Alkmaar to see the weder op bour. Came in Hilversum by 12:30.

February 7

Went to see Br. Sis. v/d Linder and Jan and Jo, also Tub and Maria. I did not feel very good. There is a spirit of contention.

February 8

Went to Sunday School, from there we went to Utrecht where I had the privilege to baptize my sister and her two daughters. It was a very fine and solemn baptismal service. Had the privilege to confer my sister as a member of the church.

February 9

Today I felt somewhat downhearted when I notice the feelings which has been created on around of my sister being baptized.

Had a splendid evening by fam. Hoogeveen, oldest daughter of Jan.

February 10

Went on the train to go back to Helder. Eat by Ewald. Spent the evening by v/d Hock, had a splendid evening. We even were brought home by car.

February 11

The wife and I went tracting for the first time. I felt glad I did. Had some conversations.

Had a very fine evening. Spent the evening by Lieinaar. Had a very fine evening.

I am sleeping better. We are having very beautiful weather. We eat by Kwast and Endjes.

February 12

Did see a notaris about a house. Hope we might be able to work out something to get our own meeting place.

Did some tracting and did see the fam. Jansen where we spent the evening. Had a very nice evening.

February 13

Today we tract for about a hour. Went to see Herman Slykerman. Then went to see v/Brummelen. Eat by Endjes and spent the evening by the O.O.V.

February 14

Spent the afternoon by Wim and Toets. Made a fine walk along the dike and harbor.

We eat by Prins and went home early.

February 15

Priesthood meeting, Sunday school. The first time the wife spoke.

We eat by fam. Leienaar, who are investigating the gospel. I have good hope they will embrace it. Had a very fine evening by fam. de Wyn.

February 16

Had a film evening about our temples. Wrote a letter to Boogaard.

February 17

Received a letter from Boogaard and I wrote one to Bill.

Spent some time bringing stuff for our new rooms.

Spent the evening by Sis. Kiesling.

February 18

Tract a hour in the morning and a hour in the afternoon. It is too darn cold. Spent the evening by van Beveren.

February 19

It is cold and am not doing much which make me feel kind of low. Spent the evening by Allen.

I don't feel very good – it is probably the winter weather.

February 20

Still cold. Stayed home during the morning. Spent evening by Brandt. Went to O.O.V.

February 21

Brought some stuff over to the new room. Spent the evening by Prins.

February 22

Had a good gospel talk with fam. Burgers. Had a good time by Buitelaar and spent the evening by Cor. Stoalman

February 23

Sunday school today. Eat vish by Sis. Kwast, very delicious had a good sacrament meeting. Spent evening by Endjes.

.February 24

Spent 2 hours by Toet, had a fairly good talk with Tine and Oma. Spent the evening by z/a Hoek. Stayed there till 11 o'clock.

February 25

Went to see the head of the weder op bouw, then to see the mayor of Helder and also a notaris. I am getting discouraged in trying to find some building. The time don't seem to be ripe for it.

Spent the evening by Keyzer.

February 26

Put a ad in the paper for our church service and took a stroll along the harbor. Eat by Sis. Kloosterman. Spent afternoon by a b. Brummelen and evening by Roll Sieverts.

It was a good day.

February 27

I took a shower and the wife ahearw ave received a letter from the Madills. Spent afternoon by Band, after that I made a walk along the harbor. Went to O.O.V.

February 28

First train to Rotterdam, missionary meeting and in the evening attended a music and song of the choir.

February 29

Sunday attended conference in the morning and in the evening. Heard some very fine talks and instructions. We eat and slept by Goud, paid a visit by Jo's room lady.

Came back with the last train.

We are going to labor in Haarlem.

March 1

Did some packing. Spent evening by Leipenan.

March 2

Did some more packing spent a very fine evening by Toets and fam.

March 3

Went to the police. Met the new missionary. Spent a fine evening by de Wyn. I am so busy every day, don't know what to do first. Got a letter from John.

March 4

Took leave from Br. Bandt who gave me a picture of him. Had a very fine evening by Jansen. Also say good by to Herman Stein and spent a pleasant hour by v. Brummelen.

March 5

Took the train to Haarlem where we met Br. Stam. Went to look for the room, which was very nice but rather expensive. Went to have a English class.

March 6

Spent nearly all day looking over the branch papers. Took a long walk with the wife. (fast day)

March 7

My first day as branch president. First priesthood meeting then Sunday school and testimony meeting. I feel loaded with responsibility. The evening meeting was well attended. Spoke for about 45 min. The wife spoke also. She start knowing how much it take to do mission work. Spent a very fine evening by Sis. Lakeweld.

March 8

Walk with the wife many hours trying to find some members. She is tired and I feel I have to slow down with her. We eat by Sis Lakeweld and by fam Haizier, where we spent the evening.

March 9

The wife stayed in bed during the morning. Brought her to the train at two o'clock. She is going to get her passport fin. Went to O.O.V., and gave a les. and administer to the mother of Sis. Lakeweld.

March 10

Did a little tracting in the morning. Went to Z.H.V. during afternoon, eat by Wilkes and talk for a number of hours with the people we have a room.

John did call from Jokohama but did not receive very good.

March 11

Got the wife from the train who has been to Apeldoorn. Took care the police and distribution. Spent the evening by Case Wilkens. I got my bike from the station.

March 12

We visit some members and went to Hoofdorp/about 9 km. Spent the evening giving English class.

March 13

Spent 3 hours on the welfare plan. Spent the afternoon and evening writing and making reports.

March 14

Sunday today. Priesthood, Sunday school and sacrament. Had a very good Sunday. We collected 291 gilder for the needy in Germany.

March 15

The is a heavy day. Has been battling with a Seven day Advent and feel kind of discouraged of my lack on knowledge. Still I feel more the truth of the gospel. Spent some time with the fam. Koster, who has a sick girl.

March 16

Spent much time with the tithing administratie

We eat by Hekking and we went to see the sick

Had an hot argument with Mr. Koster, who is very much in the spirit of rebellion

We administer to his daughter.

Went to O.O.V.

March 17

President Stam was with us till noon. We had a good class and we all used lunch together. We went to Z.H.V. Spent a fine evening by Mulder, Kl Heiligland 70. We eat by Wilkes.

March 18

We visit many members who are not of the strongest.

Went to Zandvoort and spent the evening by E. v. Komen.

March 19

Visit Sis Bos. We had very bad weather, we got plenty wet, had English class and genealogy class.

Spent much time fixing the month reports.

March 20

Today is Saturday. I went on the bike to Ymuiden to visit one of our members. Saw a troop ship come in, with troops from India

Spent all afternoon digging on our welfare project.

Nelly Beuk paid us a visit.

March 21

Priesthood meeting Sunday school sacrament meeting which was well attended. We had a Z.H.V. program which was very good. Spend the evening by Sis. Lakeweld where we met Sis. de Vries.

March 22

Spent many hours on the bike today. Visiting members. Went to Bever wyk ann Wyk dan Zee. Had a fine ride, was a good day.

March 23

Paid a visit by Aunt Allie just talking about nothing. Administer again to Tiny Koster who is very ill.

March 24

We went to Sis. Dikkeboom who has had a stroke and I administer to her. Again we went to see Tine Koster. I am worried about her sickness but I know the Lord can heal her. Spent the evening by Sis. Allebes.

March 25

Did a couple of hours tracting and spent 2 and one half hours digging on our land for the welfare.

Spent the evening by Case Wilkes. I was tired. Got a brief from Bill all is well.

March 26

Spent again 2 and one half hours on our farmland. Visit the sick again. Tine Koster is not doing as well as we hoped for. We have fast day and are praying continually. Went to genealogy and English class.

March 27

Made ready in the morning for Hilversum where we went to at noon. Went to see Jan in the hospital. Paid a visit by Staalman and Beuk and by Trits. Spent the evening up home.

March 28

Went early to Amsterdam for priesthood meeting, then the morning session of the conference where I happen to be the first speaker. The wife and eat our lunch in church and I was called on to administer to Sister Molenaar. Then the wife and I spent a couple of hours in Ryks Museum. Evening meeting was good. Went each to Haarlem.

March 29

Had a bicycle ride to Noordwyk. Party was 22 persons had a very fine time. Rode about 40 km. Every thing went fine. Paid a short visit by Sister Dikkeboom who has had a light stroke.

March 30

We tract 1 and one half hour not much success but am glad we went out. We eat by Fam. Koster had a good talk with Br. Koster who is usually inclined to criticize. His daughter is getting better now. Had a good talk with Br. Hekking.

March 31

We tract about one hour. I feel kind of sick, and the weather is chilly.

Went to see the sick in the hospital, went to bed early.

April 1

I am feeling low and would like to stay in bed. Wrote a couple of letters. One to Madill and one to the Bishop. Stayed in the house most of the day.

April 2

Visit some old members. Weather is cold and windy. I feel sick and want to go to bed. Good night.

April 3

Stayed in the room all day. I trying to get well again.

April 4

Today one year from home, supposed to be half of my mission.

Pray the Lord daily to help me to do better and become more able.

The wife and I are in the position to do much good if we just will see and use our opportunities.

Today the regular meetings which kept me busy all day. Went to bed early.

April 5

Sick in the room.

April 6

Visit some members and took sick again. Went to bed and had a high fever. Stayed in bed and called a doctor.

April 7

Felt very sick with terrible headache. Took some pills who were not the right kind.

April 8

Sick in bed.

April 9

Sick in bed.

April 10

Sick in bed.

April 11

Sick in bed. The wife went to see the old folks who are 57 years married.

April 12

Sick in bed, got a blood test which showed I had malaria, got the right kind of pills this time. Nel and Simon paid me a visit. President Zappy came over and administer to me.

April 13

Start feeling better, fever is past. Wrote a letter to Br. Bandt who is just baptized.

April 14

Start eating good again. Doctor told me to stay in for a few days.

Wrote a letter to v. Brummelen.

April 15

Still staying in the room, gets up with administrate.

April 16

Still in the room.

April 17

First day up made a nice bike ride to the shore of Bloemendaal along the shore to Ymuiden and back to Haarlem. We were plenty tired.

April 18

Regular Sunday meeting. I feel still plenty weak.

April 19

Visit all day long. The members of the branch went to Beverwyk and Wyk aan Zee. Had a very busy day got a letter from Bill.

April 20

Visit a number of member and did 4 hours administrative work. Br. Sis Stam left for home.

April 21

Had very busy day. Got our spuds plant ed. Spread the invitations for our special meeting. We are tired.

April 22

Spent most the day spreading pamphlets for our special meeting.

April 23

I feel very grateful. Tonight we had our special meeting which was not very successful. Weather was bad. Br. Siphema and Vlam spoke

April 24

Wrote letters and did administrative work.

Went to Beverwyk to visit the fam Seben, had a fine evening.

April 25

Sunday regular meetings. Had busy day. Haardvium avond in our room. 17 attendance.

April 26

Made out reports. Visit members and investigators.

April 27

Wrote a letter to John and rode around a lot today but did not do much.

April 28

Went to Z.H.V. trying to reorganize. There is a feeling of disharmony among the members.

April 29

Kermis von de deur, we are not doing much.

April 30

We are not doing much, it seems like I can't get going.

May 1

Stayed in the room biggest part of the day took a ride to the shore at Bloemendaal.

May 2

Regular meetings today had a fine Hoandviurovorde. I feel tired.

May 3

Did 2 hours trackting, felt good about it. Bought 40 K G Kunstmest for our land. Went to Beverwyk and administer to the Sis v. Seben. Spent the evening Flanrsier.

May 4

Still tryng to organize Z.H.V. 8 p.m. 2 min silence to honor war dead. Went to O.O.V.

May 5

Bought phosphate for the land. Studied a couple of hours, wrote letter to Granger and Ottalyne. Today liberation day.

May 6

Hemelsvaart day. Went with 23 of the branch to play and have a good time. Were very tired in the evening but had a good day.

May 7

We hardly can move because our legs are stiff from playing yesterday. I am feeling down hearted as I am in disagreement with myself.

May 8

Took the train to Hilversum to visit the folks. Then went Apeldoorn where we had good visit. Went to see the fam.Tykstia. Back to Haarlem.

May 9

This was not a pretty day. The spirit wasn't there. There is disharmony in the Branch moeders dag.

May 10

We went to Amsterdam on our bikes to see Br. Vlam and to put our problems before him. He gave us some fine advice.

May 11

We tract 2 hours today. The wife went alone to the doors and she enjoyed it.

May 12

Not much done today. We saw Br. and Sis. Montfrans who are on a visit today.
   I installed a new Z.H.V. bestuir.

May 13

Tract 1 and one half hour. Visit some members.

May 14

Went again tracting and had some fine talks and am invited back.
   Made a nice trip on the bike along the seashore.

May 15

Went to R.Dam for the conference. Sat 6 hours in the meetings. Did enjoy a fine spirit. Br. Lonne was with us.

May 16

Conference today. Morning was a fine festival, music, song and deelamatic.
   Spent the night by fam. Meleart.

May 17

Spent nearly all day by Geert Merinavhum. Went back to Haarlem and spent the evening by Sakerveld. One of her daughters is engaged.

May 18

Visit some member, went to O.O.V. Pres. Vlam was paying us a visit.

May 19

Did a lot of running around. We work a couple of hours on our welfare project. The spuds are coming fine.

May 20

Went to see some investigators. It was a long day. The new missionaries has arrived. Hope we will work together in harmony. Visit fam. v. Staveren and fam. Mulder.

May 21

Not much today. I don't feel like we have done our duty.

May 22

Went to Hoofdorp to see Sis. Mol. Then we went to Aalsmeer to pay a visit to my sister Nel and Simon. After coming back I went to the shore to see our scouts.

May 23

Regular Sunday meeting. We eat by Bergoma. I went again to the shore to see about our scouts. Spent the evening by Sakervelt.

May 24

Today I spent most the time studying. Spent evening by Plaijier.

May 25

Went to see some members, had some fine talks. Had a rehearsal for the O.O.V.

May 26

Went to the Z.H.V. Spent one hour welfare work. Spent the evening by fam. Bie.

May 27

Missionary meeting in Amsterdam. On our bikes, the wife and I went to Amsterdam. Then from there to Beverwyk along the canal where we had a fine evening by fam van Zeben. Came home late and tired.

May 28

The wife being tired from all the traveling we did yesterday, stayed home. I did some Branch work.

May 29

Saturday today. We went to the sea at Bloemendaal and cycled all along the shore. Spent the evening with the fam. Herrgeveld.

May 30

Sunday today. Had a good Sunday School and also a good sacrament meeting. Spent evening by Lakerveld.

May 31

Did some Branch work in the morning. Went to Ymniden and from there to Wyk aan Sea, where we met Br. Vlam. Had a fine evening.

June 1

We visit 6 fam today. Spent the evening by Bergsma.

June 2

Tract for about a hour. Spent afternoon Z.H.V. We eat by Playzier and had a long evening by investigators. Came home late.

June 3

Tract again a hour. Pres. Vlam came to visit us. Eat by Cas Wilkes. Spent evening by investigators.

June 4

Tract 1 and one half hours had some fine conversations. That's all for today.

June 5

Made a nice little trip on the bike to the shore. Went to a Youth of Christ meeting but was disappointed.

June 6

Fine meeting today. Pres. Vlam came during priesthood meeting. It was a pleasure for me to see the fam Dykstra in the meeting. I ordained Br. Wilkes to priest and set aside some sisters.

June 7

Got a other attack of fever and went to bed.

June 8

Kept myself under the blankets to get over the fever.

June 9

Stayed in bed the best part of the day. Went to the O.O.V. closing night. Nice little program.

June 10

Went tracting a while. Spent evening by fam. Ispelen. Wrote Jo a letter.

June 11

Spent the morning trying to get our spuds spread for the Colorado Kever.

Spent the evening by Dikkeboom with some investigators. Had a fine evening.

June 12

We went on the bike to the fam. Dykstra Amsterdam Noord.

We had a very fine day although the opportunity to speak about the gospel was not very great. We left again by 9 p.m. and arrived in Haarlem by 11 p.m.

June 13

Regular Sunday. I am always glad when the meeting are past. It gives me always some worries. Made a trip on our bikes to Zandvoort Bloemendaal. We enjoy our bikes very much. Weather is warm.

June 14

Went to Wyk aan Zee and spent all night with the fam Klyn. Wa. Br. Vlam and I administer to their girl. Came home by lf.

June 15

Had a very busy day. Spent about 5 hours by investigators. Did tract 1 hour. We were very tired when we came home.

June 16

Spent 4 hours on our welfare plan which made me plenty tired.

June 17

Went tracting in the morning and spent the afternoon on our land again. Came home and sit with the landlord and talk a couple of hours.

June 18

Did some Branch work. Pres. Vlam came and eat with us and at 4:30 we left on the bike for Hilversum where we arrived at 8:30.

June 19

Spent this day home and celebrated Mother's birthday – 76. Nearly all the fam was home. Went back to Haarlem 10:00 p.m. We arrived there 1:30 Sunday morning. We were pretty tired.

June 20

Regular Sunday service. Had Pres Vlam with us all day. Had some fine meetings.

Spent some time by Koster. Spent evening by Bergsma.

June 21

Spent lots of time on my monthly report and got the tithing list enz fixed up.

June 22

We tract 3 hours today. Felt pretty good about it. Had some good conversations.

June 23

Spent 6 hours drop tracting. I have a special meeting coming up and am worried about it. Spent 2 hours on our welfare project.

June 24

Today District meeting. Went to Amsterdam. Pres. Zappy was there. I did not feel very satisfied and can't say I have been built up.

Went back to Haarlem with their car. Went to Beverwyk where we spent the evening by fam Zeben.

June 25

Again did about 4 hours drop tracting. Had a special meeting this evening, which was attended by about 55 people. I was relieved when it was over. Spoke with the fam Hengeveld until 12:30.

June 26

I felt very much upset. Sometimes it is very difficult for me to get over it.

Went to Amsterdam for a couple of hours. Did a little vishing. Vader and Moeder were there too.

June 27

Regular Sunday meeting. Br. and Sis. Bruin were with us this day. Our two co-workers didn't show up at all at the evening meeting. I felt perturbed.

June 28

I felt getting sick again. I feel down.

June 29

Felt sick. Had fever and went to bed.

June 30

Stayed in bed. Received a nice letter from Bill and from Ottalyne

July 1

Stayed in bed.

July 2

Still in bed.

July 3

Out of bed but stay in the house. Wrote a letter to Bill also one to R. Paul. Made a nice ride on the bike to Ymniden over to Strand to Bloemendaal, tiring.

July 4

Had 5 meetings today which were all good attended. Stayed all afternoon by Koster and sang with the family many songs. Pr. Vlam was with us in the evening meeting.

July 5

Did some welfare work. Spent evening my investigators and did not feel very satisfied. I feel my inability to direct the conversation. I also feel again the necessity to humble oneself before going out.

July 6

Did some branch work, fix some chairs in our meeting hall. Spent evening by investigators. We had a very pleasant evening. I felt very thankful.

July 7

Took early train to Apeldoorn to see the wife's parents as it was her dad's birthday. As always we felt a spirit of resentment as far as talking about the gospel goes. It always leaves a feeling of dissatisfaction.

Went to see Oom Piet and the fam. Borkwig.

July 8

Came back from Apeldoorn, weather is very bad, received letters from Pres. Zappy about keeping the rules of the mission, which is not always easy.

July 9

Went tracting. Had a long talk with a apostate.

Visit some of our members and called it a day.

July 10

Glad it is Saturday. Am free to do what we like. Took a nice long ride on the bike. Weather is still bad.

July 11

Sunday as usual attend meetings. The wife and I spoke in the evening meeting. But we don't feel very satisfied. We are living in a spiritual turmoil. It worries me.

July 12

Much rain today. Did not go out tracting. Went to Wyk and Zee on our bikes. We got plenty wet. Had pleasant time with fam. Klyn.

We received a fine letter from Bill. He has had a wonderful furlough. He is madly in love. God bless him.

July 13

Rain, rain and lots of it. Went to see some old members.

This night I conducted the O.O.V. class. I feel like it was successful. Started to give talk about God's covenant race.

July 14

Went out tracting had some good talks. Went to Z.H.V. Eat by Plaizier and went to a investigator, had a fairly good evening. Came home late and tired.

July 15

Just did not much.

July 16

Visit some members, but weather is bad.

July 17

Took a nice ride on the bike in the morning. Went to Hoofdorp the rest of the day, had a good day b fam. Mol.

July 18

Regular Sunday service keep me busy all day. Went with Br. v Komen to Amsterdam to see his place of business. Br. and Sis Bruin came to speak.

July 19

Today I am keeping myself busy making reports. Raining again.

July 20

We made today with the Z.H.V. a very fine bus trip to the province of Bralant. We had a very good time, have been sitting 10 hours in the bus.

July 21

We went tracting, not much success.

Went to Zandvoort during the evening to fam. v. Komen.

July 22

Not much doing today. I am feeling down hearted. Went to Beverwyk to see fam. v. Zeben.

July 23

Tract about two hours, had some fine conversations. Spent some time making reports. Spent evening by Dikkeboom.

July 24

Took a nice bike ride to zantfoort, Bloemendaal enz. Went to Hoofdorp to the fam. Mol and spent the evening there.

July 25

July 26

Today Sunday, as usual, our regular meetings. I am worried always and it makes me feel tired and in a way unfit to do good missionary work..

July 27

The wife is not feeling well today and stayed in bed til 4 in the afternoon. I am just monkeying around the house.

Went to Wyk and Zee and spent the evening there. Fam. Klyn.

July 28

Tract a couple of hours. It is very hot today. Went to Z.H.V.

Spent the evening by fam. Slavinga had a very nice talk with Br. the Waal who is blind.

July 29

Went on our bikes to Amsterdam to a missionary meeting, after which we went to datis. We enjoyed us very much. Came back on our bikes by 8 o'clock.

July 30

Did some branch work. Pres. Vlam paid us a visit. We both went to see the fam. van Wyk, whose boy is going to be baptized. Spent time on the volkstelling.

July 31

The wife and I went on our bikes to fam Dylestra, where we spent some hours and where we eat. His 84 old mother was there and I was glad to meet her.

Attended a baptismal service in Amsterdam. I had the privilege to confirm Sis. Koster.

Went to Schiphol to see some planes coming in. Went back to Haarlem through the Meer.

August 1

Today we had our regular Sunday fast meeting. This was busy day and I am glad as the day is over.

August 2

Spent some hours with the church census.

August 3

Spent some more time visiting members went to Amsterdam for O.O.V. Received a letter from Boog.

August 4

Did some branch work, but I am not as active as I should be. I don't feel satisfied, am praying the Lord to do better.

August 5

Went on a outing with the Sunday School to Volkinveen. We had a very pleasant day. Everything has gone right. There was 33 in the group.

August 6

Went tracting about 2 hours, visit some members. We feel stiff in our legs from all the playing we have done yesterday.

August 7

Saturday today. Stayed home nearly all day and made a ride on the bike in the evening.

August 8

Regular Sunday meetings. Had Br. Lipkema and Br. Higbee and Hart in our evening meeting. Very bad weather today.

August 9

Received a letter from Ruel Powell. I am very pleased. Went to Wyk and Zee to visit fam. Klyn.

August 10

Received a package from Boog and something included from Bill. Did some running around. The wife is not feeling well, stayed in bed all day.

August 11

Again I got a attack of malaria, went to bed.

August 12

Sick. It rained as I have seldom seen it.

August 13

Getting better again.

August 14

Went on the bike to Hoofdorp, administer to baby fam Emil Sakerveld.

Went to Beverwyk in the evening because this city is celebrating their 650 year existence. Came back very late.

August 15

Regular Sunday meetings. We had Br. and Sis. Lipkema as speaker also Br. Higbee.

August 16

Not doing much.

August 17

Visit some members and prepare for the evening O.O.V. class. We are giving lesson out the book God's Covenant Race. Wife got sick today.

August 18

We started today digging spuds, had a good start this day.

August 19

Digging spuds, welfare.

August 20

Still in the spuds, cooperation could be better.

August 21

Spent part of the day on our welfare project, I feel tired.

August 22

Regular Sunday meetings. Pres. Zappy and his wife paid us an unexpected visit, had a good attendance.

August 23

Spent some more time welfare work. Weather is not very favorable.

August 24

Spent time making arrangements to move our crop.

August 25

Today we finished our welfare work and got the spuds send to the Haag. Had about 3000 Kg. or 3 ton. I am glad this is over.

August 26

Did not do much today, wife is still sick. Went to fam. v. Zeben. Br. Young and I administer to Sis. Nap.

August 27

Went to Amsterdam for district meeting. Prs. Zappy was present. I feel not as I should, haven't got the spirit.

Had a meeting late in the evening about getting instructions for keeping the records, came home late.

August 28

Spent day monkey around, wife still in bed.

August 29

Regular Sunday meeting, made a little ride with some of the young folks of the branch. Evening meeting was not very successful.

August 30

Wife went on the road again. Visit some members, paid also a visit to Aunt Ali. We met her oldest daughter after many years.

August 31

Today Queen's birthday, went with a group to the park and played nearly all day.

September 1

Went to Z.H.V. did some branch work.

September 2

Tract about 1and one half hour, regular missionary work.

September 3

There is quite a bit of trouble with our two partner missionaries who are not obeying the rules of the mission. It worries me quite a bit.

September 4

Saturday, spent most the day home.

September 5

Regular fast Sunday, it has been a very busy day.

September 6

Today we went to Amsterdam to see the Queen's parade, it was lucky for us that the parade past along the church. So we had a front seat. It was indeed a beautiful sight. Went on our bikes to Hilversum, had a very pleasant ride.

Eat by my sister Anna. Went to firework in the evening.

September 7

Visit sister Mon who is making ready for Zion. Spent the day visiting some relatives.

September 8

We spent the morning home, left home on our bikes to Haarlem, where we arrived at six in the evening, pretty tired.

September 9

Pres. Vlam came early in the morning and straightened out some problems. We had just lufel together, visit some members.

I am trying to reorganize the different organizations.

September 10

Spent evening by Meulmeister who is apostolish – not doing much.

September 11

Today Saturday, Sjaah Beuk came paying us a visit. We went on our bikes to Velse Ymuiden and along the seashore back over Bloemendaal, had a very nice day.

September 12

Today was a very busy day for I had to speak and had to reorganize the different organizations. I was glad when it was over.

September 13

Went to Beverwyk where we were to do some tracting but we never got that far, went Wyk an Zee.

September 14

Stayed home nearly all day, kept O.O.V. class in the evening.

September 15

Wife went to Apeldoorn to visit her folks, Mother's birthday.

September 16

Went tracting alone and made the biggest day in tracting so far, 5 hours, I felt very good about it.

September 17

Tract a couple of hours, went in the evening to Bevernwyk to visit fam. v. Zeben.

September 18

Just did not much except administrative work and genealogy class.

September 19

Sunday as usual, the different meetings, it was a busy day. The wife spoke for 15 min.

September 20

Just kept busy with branch affairs, visit investigators.

September 21

Tract some time today, spent evening in class.

September 22

Tract some hours, went to Z.H.V. visit a investigator and had a busy day.

September 23

Not much doing, some day I don't feel like doing much, wrote some letter, spent evening by fam. Helstein, who are Jehovah's Witnesses.

September 24

I don't remember, I got behind in keeping record, only we had a good genealogy class.

September 25

Our free day, went to Aalsmeer, spent some hours with Sis. Nelly, spent evening by fam. Mol at Hoofdorp.

September 26

Today Sunday, Pres. Vlam was with us in the evening meeting, made a nice walk with him during the afternoon. He spoke the whole evening meeting.

September 27

Tract 2 hours, open up a new area, spent evening by fam. Spronk who are a fine fam. and are anxious to hear the gospel.

September 28

Tract one hour, not much success, but we always are glad when we do some tracting. I spent the afternoon by Von Straveren and had a fine opportunity to explain word of wisdom. Had our opening O.O.V. evening.

September 29

Tract again 2 hours, spent afternoon with Z.H.V., paid a visit by v. Komen in Zandvoort, and spent the evening by fam. v. Looy.

September 30

We really didn't do much today. I take a shower, visit a couple of members and I went to a lecture of the "British Israel," which was very interested.

October 1

Study all morning, spent a couple of hours in the archive to find names, had a genealogy class.

October 2

Went to a meeting of all branch and district pres and pending pres in Rotterdam. We received instructions about unity in our work. Spent an hour to see Jo who is not in very good health.

October 3

Today is busy day, attend 5 meetings, spent evening by Kosben on account of a birthday party.

October 4

I am just going up in the air for genealogy work. I am spending every minute tracing out names of my people, spent evening by fam Bos investigator.

October 5

Went tracting a couple of hours, spent again some time in the archive, went to O.O.V.

October 6

Tract a few hours, went to Z.H.V. and spent some more time in the archive.

October 7

I am reading a book which make me feel entirely different. This book opens my eyes and point the way to a more happy life.

October 8

I spent all day tracing out names. I am just nuts about genealogy. I am realizing the time is getting short. I take the lead in the genealogy class.

October 9

Went to Amsterdam for a district meeting, spent 5 hours in two meetings which were very inspirational. I did enjoy the given testimonies very much. Paid a visit in the evening by fam Sponek, spoke to Hengiveld until one o'clock.

October 10

Went to Amsterdam Noord, where we held conference, which was well attended. I spoke about 10 minutes. Stayed with the Dykstra fam till next morning. We spoke together till 2 in the morning.

October 11

Got back to Haarlem, visit some peoples, went to Wyk aan Zee and had a fine profitable evening.

October 12

We went out tracting for about 2 hours, went to investigators.

October 13

Spent time in the archive to look for names, I am very much enthused for genealogical work, went to Zantvoort and to a fam Spronk.

October 14

Spent nearly all day in the archive looking for names.

October 15

Spent some more time in the archive, went to genealogy class.

October 16

Spent morning in Ryks archive, rest of the day fixing papers, made a little ride with the wife on the bike.

October 17

Had a very busy Sunday, spoke about 30 min, did not feel very good about it, had a pleasant evening by Sakervela.

October 18

Spent time again in archives. Pres. Vlam an Uffens came to pay a visit, wife made us a nice rystable.

October 19

Rain in the morning, had much writing to do.

October 20

Spent time Ryks archive looking for names, went to Z.H.V., spent evening by Onderzoekers, had a very pleasant evening.

October 21

Spent more time looking for names, went to Beverwyk, had pleasant evening by v. Zeben.

October 22

Spent all day Ryks archive, went to genealogy class.

October 23

Spent the morning archive, rest of the day working out the names. Spent the evening with Hengevela and kept on talking until 2:30 in the morning.

October 24

Regular Sunday service, we made a long day, we had some good meetings.

October 25

Went again to the archive and found some more names, spent a pleasant evening by investigators by Dikkerboom.

October 26

More genealogy today, I am afraid I am neglecting my missionary work but I am just full desire to keep going.

October 27

Monkey around quite a bit, spent evening by investigators.

October 28

Went to Amsterdam, district meeting where we listen to the counsel of Pres. Zappy, spent the evening by faber.

October 29

Went to funeral of a aunt of the wife in Amsterdam, met von Piet, father Wachter and Jo.

October 30

Today our O.O.V. gave a proparrgande evening, which went off very fine. I was very thankful.

October 31

Regular Sunday meeting, I did not feel as I should. Sometimes I am bothered by the spirit which sometime prevails among some of our members. It made me feel disgusted at times.

November 1

Went to the archive for a couple of hours, spent evening by Klyn, who are very good to us.

November 2

Visit some fam. who are sick, spent some time in the archive, went to O.O.V. and gave the les.

November 3

Went to Z.H.V. spent evening by investigators who are living by Dikkeboorn.

November 4

Bad weather, Pres. Uffens came to visit us all afternoon, spent 7 hours with investigators.

November 5

Spent time in archive, had a very good genealogy class.

November 6

Spent morning in archive, afternoon fixing sheets, fast day today.

November 7

Today one of the busiest days of my mission, I attended 6 meetings, most of them I had lead, had a fine fireside meeting by fam. Spronk.
  Anna Laherveld died today.

November 8

Went to Hilversum to celebrate Father's birthday who is 81 today, nearly all the br. and sis were home.

November 9

Spent some time with Anna and her fam., had a good chance to preach the gospel.
  Went back to Haarlem and had a O.O.V. class, spent some time with the fam. Sokerveld.

November 10

Visit some families, Z.H.V. in the afternoon, went to Zandvoort, went to investigators Zonn.

November 11

Went with Pres. Uffens to Ymniden in Beverwyk, had a fine day.

November 12

I am feeling not so well, need more rest. I am concerned about the special meeting we are going to have.

November 13

Did some archive work, Sjoah Beuk came to pay us a visit. We walk around till I got tired.

November 14

Regular Sunday Service, this is for me always a strenuous day and I am glad when it is over.

November 15

I feel sick and stayed in bed until noon, spent a little time in the archive, spent evening by Plaizion.

November 16

Still feel not so well, had a O.O.V. meeting which is getting along fine.

November 17

Regular Z.H.V. meeting, spent some time spreading pamphlets.

November 18

Spent again time for genealogy and spread some more pamphlets.

November 19

Today we will have a public meeting. It does give me some worry. Br. Rooshof and Uffens will be the speakers.

November 20

The attendance on our meeting last night was not so hot, however, the members did support us well.

We went to see my sis. Nell, had nice ride on our bikes, paid a short visit by fam Mol.

November 21

Regular Sunday meetings Pres. Uffens was with us, had a good meeting. We had a fireside meeting and the wife's birthday party, and had a swell time.

November 22

Today Br. Pronk who is a member of our branch died. I spent quite a bit of time to help them.

Received a package from Boogaard and a letter from Bill.

November 23

Did not as much today, had our O.O.V. meeting, that's all.

November 24

Z.H.V. meeting with Hoofdbestuir, went to Zandvoort and after to fam Spronck had a fine evening.

November 25

Went to Amsterdam for a Thanksgiving dinner which, by the way was a total flop, I am sorry to say.

Went to a Yschow and that was not so hot either, went home and went to bed.

November 26

Had to attend a funeral of Br. Pronk, 74, this was the first time I had to speak on a funeral. This was a new experience for me. We had a Z.H.V. bazaar in the evening.

November 27

Spent most of the day writing, and visit in the evening fam. Ispelen.

November 28

Regular Sunday meeting, had to speak 30 min, Haarvuin evening by Bergsman.

November 29

Went in the afternoon to the daughter of Boogaard who is living in Bergen. We had a good evening.

November 30

Visit different people who are sick, the O.O.V. was very good.

December 1

Z.H.V. meeting today, had a investigator coming to our room. I hope I might have done some good. We are getting busy for our anniversary

December 2

Did some research work at the archives, spent evening by fam. Faber, who are very kind to us. Received a nice letter from Ruel Paul also 12 dollars.

December 3

Had a good genealogy class. The weather was bad and as I came home I had to go out to render service to a br. who is in distress and I prayed the Lord that I indeed may be a instrument in his hand to do what is right. Received a package from Katrien.

December 4

Regular Saturday, wrote some letters and we had St. Nicolas in the evening. Received a package from John D. Hill.

December 5

Regular Sunday, had a very busy Sunday and was very tired in the evening.

December 6

Went to see my sister Nel, who is quite ill lately. I spent a very fine evening as I had a wonderful opportunity to explain the gospel, hope I have done some good.

December 7

Had our O.O.V. which was very good, had some very good talks, I felt thankful. The wife is getting busy for our wedding anniversary.

December 8

Just did some visiting, trying to do some good, spent evening by Lakerveld, had a very fine evening.

December 9

Travel around to visit people, spent evening by Stevens.

December 10

Been busy making preparation for our 25 year wedding day. It takes quite a bit of work and planning. We had a very good genealogy class. Stayed up very late making crocket.

December 11

Today the big day, are very busy all day. Father, Mother, one brother, 5 sisters and 4 brother-in-law attended our party. We had about 65 people and I am very thankful for everything.

December 12

Regular Sunday school. We had very fine fire-side meeting. We enjoyed it very much.

December 13

Clean up something of our party, went to investigators fam Makely.

December 14

We don't do much any more in the day time, went to O.O.V., where we had a very pleasant time.

December 15

Did some things pertaining to branch work, spent afternoon together with the wife play-ing with the children on our jonght work, had a very splendid evening by investgator Sis. Allebes.

December 16

Left this morning for Aalsmeer to see my sister. I found her and Vim in a much better spiritual condition of which I am very glad. We stayed there the night.

December 17

Came back from Aalsmeer at noon and paid a visit by fam Lakerfeld.

December 18

Regular Saturday, spent a couple of hours writing.

December 19

Regular Sunday, I had a bad day, but that's all in a day's work. I spoke about a half hour.

December 20

Did all day administration work, spent evening by Klyn in Beverwyk, kept on figuring until two o'clock.

December 21

More figuring and making reports, went to Amsterdam to see Uffens, went to O.O.V.

December 22

Spent afternoon with the youth, evening by Spronk.

December 23

Went to Amsterdam to have our Xmas dinner, had a nice day.

December 24

Spent evening by Hevjveld

December 25

Spent most of the day making ready for Xmas, had our party in the afternoon which wasn't too much to brag about.

December 26

Regular Sunday service, it is getting very difficult for me to speak in the meetings and at times I feel downhearted.

December 27

Monday is my low day as I don't feel like doing anything except writing and reading. I went to a investigator, but did not feel I have done any good.

December 28

Regular O.O.V., we made a fine evening of it.

December 29

Youth work, made ready for our short vacation.

December 30

Went to Apeldoorn and stayed there a couple days, spent my days mostly reading magazines.

December 31

Last day of the year, had a good old and new, one more year gone never to come back again.

1949

January 1

Went Hilversum to see the folks, spent time by Anna, went back to Haarlem same evening.

January 2

Sunday and these are becoming more and more a burden on account of the speaking. It seems like I am getting worse collecting my thoughts. I spoke about a half hour. Wife is sick today.

January 3

Wife still sick. I spent evening with investigators Stevens, who gave me his whole life story and the trouble he has got himself in. We prayed together and we will fast.

January 4

Spent some time looking up different members, stayed with de wife the afternoon. She is still sick. Had O.O.V. in the evening. I went to see some relations in the far distance but could not get much information out of him. He lives in Santpoort.

January 5

Had youth work today, went to eat by Hekking, spent the evening by von Ispelen, stayed up late by Hengeveld.

January 6

Went to see Pres. Uffens about branch matters, stayed with the wife afternoon, she is still sick.

January 7

I am feeling down a little. Visit a few members, spent time by fam Spronk, went to genealogy class, but only 3 people were there.

January 8

Saturday, stayed home nearly all day, felt pretty sick.

January 9

Regular Sunday, I had charge of the Sunday school, also in the evening meeting I had to speak 45 minutes, went to investigators fam. Stevens.

January 10

Went to salf Sis. Klop meiger, visit some more members, spent evening by Stavinger.

January 11

Went to station to see Pres. Uffens but he never showed up, went to O.O.V. and paid a visit to fam. Spronk.

January 12

Went with Pres. Uffens to Ymninden to visit some people, we had a very nice day. Had investigators visiting us all evening. Wife is getting better again.

January 13

Went to Beverwyk, visit fam. v. Zeben, eat there with them and went to a show about Thilps and Steel ovens by Ymniden. It was very interesting.

January 14

Wife went to see a doctor for a check up, there is something wrong with her. I am feeling kind of downhearted, but will get over it. Had a genealogy class in the evening.

January 15

Today I had the privilege to baptize fam. Spronk. I feel greatly blessed.

January 16

Today Sunday, had our regular meetings. Sunday school was very nice, also our sacrament meeting. We had 3 bro. from headquarters to speak to us. Spent the evening by Sakerveld.

January 17

Monkey around a bit, Pres. Zappy came to see us and told us to go back home 25 March. I felt kind of glad although I cannot realize that the end of my mission is near. Spent evening by fam. Booms and came v. Melser.

January 18

Eat by fam. Brown and by Bergoma, went to O.O.V. and did call on fam. von Ispelen.

January 19

Made the monthly reports, eat by Wilds, went to the Primary, spent evening by fam. Alleges, had a very nice evening.

January 20

Had a good talk with Olders, where I did eat, spent some time by fam van Staveren, spent evening by Dikkerboom.

January 21

Look a bad, eat in our room, had a nice boiled vish, had our genealogy class.

January 22

Made a very nice trip on the bike with the wife. It was beautiful weather and we rode to Sandvoort along the shore, spent rest of day writing letters.

January 23

Regular Sunday service, Pres. Uffens was with us all day. Had a good Sunday school and evening meeting, had a fireside meeting at our place on account of my birthday. We made some pictures.

January 24

Today it was my lot to give a talk at a funeral. This not a easy thing to do, but it went along alright. Did not do much the rest of the day, had Cor and Martha visiting us, received a letter from Bill.

January 25

Did not do much today. We went to O.O.V., went to Amsterdam to see Bro. van Komen so he would come to speak to us on Sunday, stayed by Bro. v. Ispelen until 1 o'clock.

January 26

Spent time to attend Primary, visit some one in the hospital, spent evening by a fam Westerhuis who are living in a boat, had a very fine evening.

January 27

Spent most of the day home reading and writing and preparing for Sunday service, spent evening by fam. Sorn, Br. and Sis Bergsman.

January 28

Rotterdam conference, special for missionaries, had two meetings and a program in the evening. We received warnings against black market dealings, spent evening by Jo. Wachter.

January 29

Again we had two meetings which were very inspirational, went back to Haarlem same evening, paid a visit to Eg. Wootenboom.

January 30

Regular Sunday meeting, eat by Koster, spent evening by v. Ispelen, came home and talk with Hengeveld until 1 o'clock.

January 31

Received 2 letters from the states, went to Alkmaar to see Br. Kwast who is very ill, went after that to berger binnen to visit the fam. Veenedaal, had a fine evening.

February 1

Visit a few members, some are laying in the hospital, went to O.O.V., received a package from Mrs. Cannon, which has been on the way for about 3 months.

February 2

Went to Primary, send letters to different members inviting them to special meeting, spent evening by investigator Fabel.

February 3

Went to Hoofdorp to visit fam. Mol, just felt it has been a lost day.

February 4

New missionary came so I had to spend some time with him showing him the way around. Had our special meeting and farewell for Pres. Vlam, we had a very nice meeting.

February 5

Study most of the day, took a new missionary around.

February 6

Fast day, attended 5 meetings, spent evening by Lakderveld, Emil's last day in Holland. He is going to the Dutch East Indies, Verodeneerd. 2 in the lower priesthood.

February 7

Spent some time with branch work, spent evening by fam. Sorn, stayed there until

12:30. Some preacher was there. I felt greatly blessed.

February 8

Went around with the two new partners, showed them our peace of land for the welfare, went to O.O.V., had a good time. Administer to the baby Lakerveld.

February 9

Bad weather in the morning, went to Z.H.V. and youth work, spent evening by Allebes. Again a splendid evening. We made it very late.

February 10

Spent a very pleasant hour by Spronk, eat by Dikkerboom and paid a visit by fam Westerhuis on the ship Nienme Sorg, had a very good time.

February 11

Had a very splendid day. Went out tracting alone and had some very fine conversations. Our genealogical class was held, although there were few of us, just fine.

February 12

Went to Amsterdam to see Uffens and to see the missionaries play ball. I then took a opportunity to see the ship museum, which was very interesting to me. Spent evening by fam van Alfen, it was very late.

February 13

Regular Sunday meetings, had a pleasant time by Spronk and von Ispelen.

February 14

Made arrangement to get work started on our land, went to Jmuiden to visit two families, had a very good time and I hope we did some good.

February 15

Visit some investigators, had a nice O.O.V.

February 16

Spent a couple of hours with the youth, evening by Allebes, who are investigators and are some fine people.

February 17

Pres. Uffens came to visit us. We had a nice couple of hours together. Went to see Sis. Bos, then we went to Wyk ann Zee to visit my sister Nel and the fam Klyn. We got home late and we made the trip on our bikes.

February 18

We had a very nice show in the evening. Br. Levi and de Boer came to run the show. Visit some people during the day.

February 19

We made a long trip on our bikes and we sure did enjoy it. Went to Aunt Alie the evening and met the whole family.

February 20

Regular Sunday, priesthood meeting and Sunday school. I had to conduct the whole meeting. Evenings we had Brother Davis and Diender to speak to us. Had a very fine fireside chat by Bram van Wyk.

February 21

Spent 3 hours for administrative, had lunch by Lakerveld, went to Ymniden on our bikes and visit Sis. Boes and the fam Annes who are investigating, came back to Haarlem on our bikes in the rain.

February 22

Visit a few fam, took care of the Primary, visit Allebes, Dikkerbloom

February 23

Went to Bevernwyk to give my farewell to fam Seben, had a fine afternoon, spent evening by fam Sorn, who is a brother of Sis. Bergsona.

February 24

Had our regular district meeting, had a very fine meal and went to Dyhstra and spent the evening there.

February 25

Start packing our belongings, visit many of the saints, went to Helder to attend funeral service of Br. Kwast, funeral was very solemn, met all the old friends.

February 26

Some more packing, went to Amsterdam to attend baptismal service for Br. Bergema, Br. Allebes, Br. v. Alphen, Br. Hekking. It was a very fine service. Spent evening by v. Alphen.

February 27

Our last Sunday, it was a very busy day and we have been blessed abundantly. Also we had very heartwarming evening, took leave of everybody. This is the end of our stay in Haarlem.

February 28

Went to Rotterdam to see the consul, get my passport fixed, went to H.A.L.M.E. to get my ticket for the boat, spent night by Jo Wachter. A real storm was blowing. We went to see Jo and Geest.

March 1

Went to see the ship museum in Rotterdam, went back to Haarlem and spent evening packing.

March 2

Went to Helder where we arrived 4:30, stayed home and had very fine gospel talk with the families.

March 3

Went around the harbor, visit a few people, spent some time by Jo Ekkys, spent even by Ewald, 12 and one half year anniversary.

March 4

Spent all day by Toets, visit some families.

March 5

Took a trip over Huisduinen, I just about froze to death, stayed home with the family.

March 6

Went to Sunday school, came back home and Wim made some morning pictures. We hope they will be alright. Went to night meeting and bore our testimony, eat by Endjes and had a nice talk with Wim.

March 7

Woke up early, got just in time the bus out Den Helder, pick up our bikes in Haarlem and rode to Aalsmeer to see Nel and Simon, stayed there a little while and rode to Hilversum, where we arrived about 5 o'clock, spent part of the evening by Anna.

March 8

Went to the Haag to see Pres. Zappy, finally we got some done, came back about 10 o'clock.

March 9

Made a nice trip on the bike, it was pretty cold, spent evening by Jean and Jur.

March 10

Again we bike around the country, we feel greatly blessed, spent evening by Anna and Souw.

March 11

Went to see Adriaan, who is in the hospital, rode around alone for many miles, spent some time by Frits and Marie.

March 12

Went to Amsterdam to attend district meeting, attended a little show in the Amsterdam ward, got back home about 11 o'clock.

March 13

Went to Amsterdam conference, I did speak about 15 min. This was my farewell to many fine members. Attended sacrament meeting in Hilversum, spoke there about 30 min. The fam. came together in the evening, but the sfeer was not very good.

March 14

Took the bike and went to Apeldoorn, had a very nice ride, found everything ok, started to do some work in the garden.

March 15

Spent most of the day working in the garden.

March 16

Weather is not so good, I don't feel so good sitting in the house. We went to spend the evening by fam. Bokhorst and we had a very fine evening and had a very fine opportunity to explain the gospel.

March 17

Still bad weather, monkey around a bit, did a lot of reading and feel like we never get a chance to speak to the folks about religion.

March 18

Rain, rain, and still more. Read, read and read some more.

March 19

Weather better and I could do some garden work, which I was glad to do. We both feel kind of disappointed because we feel a great gulf between us and our parents.

March 20

Today is Sunday. I went with the wife to Sunday school. We met with a br. who has been a preacher and became a member of the church. We attended night meeting I spoke about 45 min. This has been the last time that I had the opportunity to preach the gospel in Holland.

March 21

We went back on our bikes from Apeldoorn to Hilversum, took us about 5 hours, spent evening by Anna, had a nice evening.

March 22

Spent most of our day home, my 5 sisters came during the afternoon together, stayed home night.

March 23

Went to Born to see A. and S. to say goodbye, went to Zwammerdam to see fam Birk, come home late.

March 24

Fixed distribution papers, called the Haage by phone to get some information about the boat, members of my fam. came to say good-bye to us.

March 25

Today the end of our mission, say good bye to our parents, which was a difficult thing to do. Three sisters went with us to see us off, got through the customs very easily, left Rotterdam 10 p.m., stayed on deck till we left Hook van Holland, then took a shower and went to bed.

March 26

Reached South Hampton about one o'clock, took up about 50 passengers and mail, left again about five p.m. and we are going to the USA, very fine weather.

March 27

Very fine weather, had a meeting together with five of us, used the sacrament and bore our testimonies.

Had a show in the evening but I could not enjoy it very much.

March 28

Very fine weather, did some deck games, day past by very fast.

March 29

Wife got sick, had to go to bed, spit in the back. Tonight we had a picture show who was a little better.

March 30

Weather pretty rough, here are quite a few passengers seasick. Did some games and did lots of reading.

March 31

Still rough, wife still in bed, spent day as usual.

April 1

Weather is fine, do lot of deck games, had a nice show in the evening, wife got up again.

April 2

Nice weather again, played a lot on deck, we sang together by the piano, make preparation for leaving.

Epilogue 1983-1988

1983

Upon approaching my 85th birthday I wonder sometimes how many more years I will be able to continue to labor in the House of the lord. This has been such an important part of the last 18 years.

Looking back upon our 59 years of married life, with all the ups and downs, there is so much we should be thankful for, so much we should remember and talk about and try to push all our failings and mistakes in the background and keep on getting an understanding of each other's needs.

This being the last chapter of my life story which covers about 65 years having written very little about our posterity I will express our thanks and gratitude for our two sons and their wives, our eight grandchildren who are at this writing (1988) between the ages of 26-37—ten fruitful years. Grateful for the three husbands and four daughters-in-law who brought together, up to this time, 27 great-grandchildren all healthy without physical blemish of which we are grateful. Hoping in due time we may introduce one more daughter-in-law when our youngest grandson may choose him a wife. It is a joy to see them grow up as fast as they do. See them develop attributes which give hope for the future of producing leaders in their chosen field. Hoping that the example of the parents and teachings they are receiving may give them the faith and understanding of the purpose of life here upon the earth. We in our old age thankful beyond words thinking of the poor and unprepared start of this marriage which according to some would not last one year (and how close they were in their opinion) it is a wonder that we be so thankful for those two fine boys who have been instruments in the hands go the Lord.

To bring to pass in the most critical time of our lives that great change with much up and down yet made this marriage last better than 64 years and has given us such faithful and progressing posterity. That all of them will hold themselves close to the Lord, willing to sacrifice for the sake of the Gospel and may enjoy the blessings of which the Lord has promised to all who will keep his commandments.

Looking back on those nearly 65 years all the experiences, all answered prayers in our behalf, all the guiding influences which has kept us faithful and willing to serve we acknowledge the hand of the Lord. Realizing the many times my life has been spared which has been promised in my Patriarchal Blessing how grateful I need to be.

Now about my wife who has loved me even in the darkest hours, even when all did look hopeless, yet believed in me never has given up this stubborn husband who wanted to fly higher than the Lord allowed him for his own good. Yet impulsive as she is, how quick she may have her judgements ready, how quick she may change her mind, yet faithful and so willing to endure and be willing to help me in anything I try to undertake I give her all the credit for whatever we have accomplished so quick to forgive and forget which for me is sometimes so hard to do.

I have directed those who have typed my history to make very few changes or corrections as I felt the objective of my history was that the reader may know me as I am.

May the Lord bless you and that you may benefit by the lessons that I have learned.

April 1988

Being the first of the Dinkelman line (as far as is known) and receiving the Restored Gospel September 1, 1927, bringing the name Dinkelman upon the register of the Church of Jesus Christ of Latter Day Saints, I feel thankful to the Lord and looking at my posterity of two sons, eight grandchildren, and 27 great grandchildren (all of who upon reaching the age of accountability have been baptized and are active) and those who have married in the family are active members. This makes me thankful to the Lord and gave me a measure of pride and made writing this, my life story, a worthwhile undertaking.

I hope this story may be of benefit to my posterity on the journey through life.

[Hendrik passed away November 22, 1988 in Salt Lake City, Utah.
Jacoba passed away January 14, 1998 in Salt Lake City, Utah.]

Index

www.ingramcontent.com/pod-product-compliance
Lightning Source LLC
Chambersburg PA
CBHW062042090426
42740CB00016B/2992